QUOTABLE SEX

QUOTABLE
SEX

CAROLE McKENZIE

ST.MARTIN'S PRESS, NEW YORK

ISBN 0-312-10529-0

First published in Great Britain by
Mainstream Publishing Company Limited.

Acknowledgments

There are many to whom I am indebted. Some are included here but, alas, others prefer to remain anonymous.

A special thanks to Alison for her enthusiastic help and encouragement, and to Carolyn Ridsdale for her interesting graphic interpretations.

Also to John for his unfailing stamina and support:

'A dynamite book.
Encourages excess sex
. . . Highly recommended.'

Carole McKenzie
September 1992

ACRONYMS

SIECUS
Sex Information and Education Council of the United States. Siecus was founded in 1964, when one in two marriages was warped by sexual problems. Sex had to be brought out of the Victorian closet – freed from the guilt and fear, bigotry and misconceptions which shrouded it, if America was to recover from its deep-rooted sexual trouble.
SIECUS fund raising letter, 1979

SINBADS
Women who are: – Single In Need of Blokes, in Absolutely Desperate State

U.S.W.I.S.O.M.W.A.G.M.O.H.O.T.M.
United Single Women In Search Of Men Who Aren't Gay, Married, Or Hung-up On Their Mothers

SCUM
Society for Cutting Up Men manifesto

ACTING

I'm glad you like my Catherine. I like her too. She ruled thirty million people and had three thousand lovers. I do the best I can in two hours.
Mae West *(1892-1980), American actress, speaking from the stage after her performance in* Catherine the Great

Dramatic art in her opinion is knowing how to fill a sweater.
Bette Davis *on Jayne Mansfield*

I just pretended I was a cartoon. I exaggerated every move. Every time I made a movement, I would think like a cartoon.
Kim Basinger, *American film star, on her role as a cartoon seductress*

All those actresses who turned the film away are stupid. I believe that if you have the right equipment and a point of view, that's a deadly combination.
Sharon Stone, *American actress, on her role in the film* Basic Instinct

Some American producers discuss actresses as if they
were a load of cows.
Jackie Collins, author

A good actress lasts, and sex attraction does not.
Brigitte Bardot

I have made enough faces.
Greta Garbo, refusing ever again to perform, c.1946

ADVICE

A man can be a great lover, but no matter how well he
performs, sex won't compensate for personality,
intelligence, consideration, and whatever else you may
be looking for. You may think you're in love when the
passions of sex get hold of you, but if you didn't love
the man before, you won't love him after. Like him,
maybe – but not love him!
Mae West

Ladies, here's a hint; if you're playing against a friend
who has big boobs, bring her to the net and make her
hit backhand volleys. That's the hardest shot for the
well-endowed.
Billie Jean King, Wimbledon tennis champion

The strongest possible piece of advice I would give to
any young woman is: don't screw around and don't
smoke.
Edwina Currie MP

Never be possessive. If a female friend lets on that she is
going out with another man, be kind and understanding. If she says she would like to go out with all
the Dallas Cowboys, including the coaching staff, the
same applies. Tell her 'Kath, you must go right ahead
and do what you feel is right'. Unless you actually care
for her, in which case you must see to it that she has no
male contact whatsoever.
*Bruce Jay Friedman, 'Sex and the Lonely Guy', Esquire magazine,
1977*

So this gentleman said a girl with brains ought to do
something else with them besides think.
Anita Loos (1891-1981), American novelist, Gentlemen Prefer
Blondes, *1928*

The only time to believe any kind of rating is when it shows you at the top.
Bob Hope, *quoted in* Playboy *magazine, 1973*

If you want something done well, get a couple of old broads to do it.
Bette Davis

You must try harder at your French letters.
TV presenter and actor **Phillip Schofield**, *advising children on writing in French*

Don't try! You have too luscious a bosom to keep the conversation general.
Madame Aubernon, *French hostess known for her salon*

In love-making, feigning lovers succeed much better than the really devoted.
Ninon de Lenclos *(1615-1705), seventeenth-century feminist and leader of Parisian society*

Men should keep their eyes wide open before marriage, and half-shut afterwards.
Madeleine de Scudery *(1607-1701), French author*

When you're bored with yourself, marry and be bored with someone else.
David Pryce-Jones, *British author and critic,* Owls and Satyrs, *1960*

You don't want to work here. After all, how many ways are there to say 'big tits'?
Shel Silverstein, *American cartoonist and songwriter*

Never hurt a man whom you respect nor a woman whom you do not deeply love.
George C. Scott, *American film star,* Esquire *magazine, 1965*

A woman seldom asks for advice until she has bought her wedding clothes.
Joseph Addison, Spectator, *1712*

Instead of getting hard ourselves and trying to compete, women should try and give their best qualities to men – bring them softness, teach them how to cry.
Joan Baez, *American folk and protest singer,* 'Sexism Seen but not Heard', Los Angeles Times, *1974*

To control a man a woman must first control herself.
Minna Antrim, *American writer*, Naked Truth and Veiled
Allusions

AFFAIRS

What I have seen of the love affairs of other people has
not led me to regret that deficiency in my experience.
George Bernard Shaw *(1856-1950), Irish dramatist, novelist and
critic*

Just how difficult it is to write a biography can be
reckoned by anybody who sits down and considers just
how many people know the real truth about his or her
love affairs.
Rebecca West *(1892-1983), British journalist and novelist*

I don't remember any love affairs. One must keep love
affairs quiet.
The Duchess of Windsor

I knew about the affair . . . I told Paddy . . . look kiddo,
you've got to come clean or people will think that it's
something much worse.
Jane Ashdown, *on her husband's much publicised affair*

Baloney!
Barbara Bush, *wife of President George Bush, on the allegations
that he had an affair*

I don't sleep with married men, but what I mean is that
I don't sleep with happily married men.
Britt Ekland, *Swedish film actress, putting the record straight*

Some of the greatest affairs I've known involved one
actor unassisted.
Wilson Mizner *(1876-1933), American dramatist and wit (attrib)*

[Americans are] better at having a love affair that lasts
ten minutes than any other people in the world.
Stephen Spender

Alex, I can't see why having an affair with someone on
and off is any worse than being married for a course or
two at mealtimes.
Penelope Gilliatt, *British writer and film critic, Sunday Bloody
Sunday*

AGEING

Now that I'm over sixty I'm veering toward respectability.
Shelley Winters, American actress

I refuse to admit that I'm more than fifty-two even if that does make my sons illegitimate.
Lady Astor

The lovely thing about being forty is that you can appreciate twenty-five-year-old men more.
Colleen McCullough

A man's as old as he's feeling, a woman as old as she looks.
Mortimer Collins (1827-76), English novelist and poet

When a woman tells you her age, it's all right to look surprised, but don't scowl.
Wilson Mizner

The age of a woman doesn't mean a thing. The best tunes are played on the oldest fiddles.
Sigmund Z. Engel

Middle age is the time when a man is always thinking that in a week or two he will feel as good as ever.
Don Marquis (1878-1937), American humorist and journalist

You know, when I first went into the movies Lionel Barrymore played my grandfather. Later he played my father and finally he played my husband. If he had lived I'm sure I would have played his mother. That's the way it is in Hollywood. The men get younger and the women get older.
Lillian Gish

The older one grows the more one likes indecency.
Virginia Woolf (1882-1941), English novelist and critic, Monday or Tuesday

I've always been a bit more maturer than what I am.
Samantha Fox, page-three model

When a woman in love reaches a certain age, though her heart may cease to sing, her eyes remain veiled with gratitude.
Colette (1873-1954), French writer

I'm forty and no woman knows what falling in love can mean until she's forty.
Marie Lloyd (1870-1922), *British music-hall singer*

The great thing about being thirty is that there are a great deal more available women. The young ones look younger and the old ones don't look nearly so old.
Glen Frey, *American rock star*

A lot of people start to fall to bits at thirty . . . quite honestly once you are able to reproduce you're over the hill. You start to go downhill at eighteen physically.
Mick Jagger, *British rock star*

Time and trouble will tame an advanced woman, but an advanced old woman is uncontrollable by any earthly force.
Dorothy L. Sayers

Every man over forty is a scoundrel.
George Bernard Shaw

She may very well pass for forty-three in the dusk, with a light behind her!
Mortimer Collins, The Unknown Quantity, *1876*

A man is only as old as the woman he feels.
Groucho Marx, *American comedian*

I have always felt that a woman has the right to treat the subject of her age with ambiguity until, perhaps, she passes into the realm of over ninety. Then it is better she be candid with herself and with the world.
Helena Rubinstein (1882-1965), *Polish-born American cosmetics manufacturer*, My Life for Beauty, *1965*

One searches the magazines in vain for women past their first youth. The middle-aged face apparently sells neither perfume nor floor wax. The role of the mature woman in the media is almost entirely negative.
Janet Harris, *American writer and educator*, The Prime of Ms America, *1975*

AIDS

Take the wife.
Edwina Currie MP advising businessmen travelling abroad on how to avoid catching AIDS

It could be said that the AIDS pandemic is a classic
own-goal scored by the human race against itself.
Princess Anne, *the Princess Royal*

Every time you sleep with a boy you sleep with all his
old girlfriends.
AIDS advertisement, 1987

The Government has decided on a birds and bees
theme. Several times a day they show a television
cartoon in which a lustful-looking bee flies from flower
to flower while a voice-over says, 'There is a disease
that spreads through sex.' At the end of the cartoon the
bee drops down dead.
   We would like to make it quite clear that bees are not
promiscuous. They do not carry AIDS. And they do not
visit flowers for sex, but for nectar.
Mr Ton Kempts, *secretary of the Dutch Bee-keepers' League,*
protesting against the Dutch Government's anti-AIDS campaign

The most frightening fact about AIDS is that it can be
spread by normal sex between men and women. This is
still rare in Scotland.
Scottish Sunday Mail

A L I M O N Y

You never realise how short a month is until you pay
alimony.
John Barrymore

If the income tax is the price you have to pay to keep
the government on its feet, alimony is the price we have
to pay for sweeping a woman off hers.
Groucho Marx

Alimony is the curse of the writing classes.
Norman Mailer

Billing minus cooing.
Mary Dorsey

The high cost of leaving.
Anon

Bounty after the mutiny
Johnny Carson on *NBC's* Tonight Show, *1984*

The claim for alimony . . . implies the assumption that a
woman is economically helpless.
Suzanne Lafollete, Concerning Women

A R T

Why should I paint dead fish, onions and beer glasses?
Girls are so much prettier.
Marie Laurencin (1885-1956), French painter, quoted in Time
magazine, 1956

A painting of a nude Mick Jagger, taken from the rear
by Cecil Beaton, was sold by London auctioneers
Bonham's yesterday for £1,050.
Report in the Evening Standard, 16 July 1986

B A D

I believe that it's better to be looked over than it is to be
overlooked. And that a girl who keeps her eyes open is
always the kind to look out for. I know the difference
between a good man and a bad one, but I haven't
decided which I like better.
Mae West

I don't think that the wrath of God descends on bad
girls. No, I think bad girls have a ball and die having a
ball. The life my characters lead – having affairs, living
from one party to the next . . . and going shopping –
this is their idea of a ball. It's not up to me to say,
'Girls, this isn't the sort of ball you should be having'.
Shobha De, bestselling Indian author

There is no worse evil than a bad woman; and nothing
has ever been produced better than a good one.
Euripides (c.480-406BC), Greek dramatist, Melanippe, fifth
century BC

It's the good girls who keep the diaries; the bad girls
never have the time.
Tallulah Bankhead (1902-68), American actress

BACHELORS

A bachelor's virtue depends upon his alertness; a
married man's depends upon his wife's.
H. L. Mencken (1880-1956), American writer and humorist

Never trust a husband too far, nor a bachelor too near.
Helen Rowland

Bachelors are not fashionable any more. They are a
damaged lot. Too much is known about them.
Oscar Wilde (1854-1900), Irish writer and dramatist, An Ideal
Husband, *1895*

Being a bachelor is the first requisite of the man who
wishes to form an ideal home.
Beverly Nichols

A bachelor never quite gets over the idea that he is a
thing of beauty and a boy forever.
Helen Rowland

A bachelor has to have inspiration for making love to a
woman, a married man needs only an excuse.
Helen Rowland

I'm o'er young, I'm o'er young,
I'm o'er young to marry yet!
I'm o'er young, 'twod be a sin
to tak me frae my mammy yet.
Robert Burns (1759-96), Scottish poet, Ay Waukin O

People always assume that bachelors are single by
choice and spinsters because nobody asked them. It
never enters their heads that poor bachelors might have
worn the knees of their trousers out proposing to girls
who rejected them or that a girl might deliberately stay
unmarried because she didn't want to spend the rest of
her life filling a man's stomach with food and washing
his dirty shirts.
Jilly Cooper, Angels in a Rush

No unmarried woman can be polite to a bachelor
without beginning to speculate how he would look in a
wedding coat. This fact, which is too obvious to need
proof, makes friendly dealings with them somewhat
strained.
H. L. Mencken

Most men are [married]. I say countries go to war. The
question is – is it a good idea? I live alone (a bachelor
flat in Teddington) and any woman would love to get
their hands on it and do it over. But I have freedom and
the only person I have to please is me.
Benny Hill

BEAUTY

For the butterfly, mating and propagation involve the
sacrifice of life; for the human being, the sacrifice of
beauty.
*Johann Wolfgang von Goethe (1749-1832), German poet,
playwright, scientist and court official*

Is it too much to ask that a woman be spared the daily
struggle for superhuman beauty in order to offer it to
the caresses of a subhumanly ugly mate?
Germaine Greer

I'm not denyin' the women are foolish: God Almighty
made 'em to match the men.
George Eliot (Mary Ann Evans, 1819-80), English novelist

I love being a woman. You can cry. You get to wear
pants now. If you're on a boat and it's going to sink,
you get to go on the rescue boat first. You can wear
cute clothes. It must be a great thing, or so many men
wouldn't be wanting to do it.
Gilda Radner

We have to have faith in ourselves. I have never met a
woman who, deep down in her core, really believes she
has great legs. And if she suspects that she might have
great legs, then she's convinced that she has a shrill
voice and no neck.
Cynthia Heimel, American journalist

There's a difference between beauty and charm. A
beautiful woman is one I notice. A charming woman is
one who notices me.
John Erskine

It's a good thing that beauty is only skin deep or I'd be
rotten to the core.
Phyllis Diller

When I go to the beauty parlour, I always use the
emergency entrance. Sometimes I just go for an
estimate.
Phyllis Diller

Character contributes to beauty. It fortifies a woman as
her youth fades.
Jacqueline Bisset, British actress

You can take no credit for beauty at sixteen. But if you
are beautiful at sixty, it will be your soul's own doing.
Marie Stopes

Beauty is altogether in the eye of the beholder.
Margaret Wolfe Hungerford (1855-97), Irish novelist, Molly
Bawn

It is better to be beautiful than to be good. But it is
better to be good than to be ugly.
Oscar Wilde

Beauty for some provides escape
Who gain happiness in eyeing the
gorgeous buttocks of the ape
or Autumn sunsets exquisitely dying.
Aldous Huxley (1894-1963), English writer

The epithet beautiful is used by surgeons to describe
operations which their patients describe as ghastly, by
physicists to describe measurement which leave
sentimentalists cold, by lawyers to describe the objects
of this infatuation, however unattractive they may
appear to the unaffected spectators.
George Bernard Shaw

Beauty is indeed a good gift of God; but that the good
may not think it a great good, God dispenses it even to
the wicked.
Saint Augustine (354-430)

Beauty. The power by which a woman charms a lover
and terrifies a husband.
Ambrose Bierce (1842-1914), American author

If beauty isn't genius it usually signals at least a high
level of animal cunning.
Peter York, British journalist

The feminine vanity-case is the grave of masculine illusions.
Helen Rowland

In the factory we make cosmetics. In the store we sell hope.
Charles Revson (1906-75), American business tycoon, Fire and Ice, *1975*

Life belongs to the pretty woman.
Lady Isobel Barnet, British television personality

One girl can be pretty – but a dozen are only a chorus.
F. Scott Fitzgerald (1896-1940), American novelist, The Last Tycoon

Manners are especially the need of the plain. The pretty can get away with anything.
Evelyn Waugh (1903-66), British novelist

My love in her attire doth show her wit.
It doth so well become her:
For every season she hath dressings fit,
for winter, spring and summer.
No beauty she doth miss,
when all her robes are on:
but beauty's self she is,
when all her robes are gone.
Anon, madrigal, sixteenth century

Shall I compare thee to a summer's day?
Thou are more lovely and more temperate.
Rough winds do shake the darling buds of May,
and summer's lease hath all too short a date.
William Shakespeare, Sonnet, 1609

You're the most beautiful woman I've ever seen, which doesn't say much for you.
Groucho Marx, American comedian, Animal Crackers, *1930*

In Britain, an attractive woman is somehow suspect. If there is talent as well, it is overshadowed. Beauty and brains just can't be entertained; someone has been too extravagant.
Vivien Leigh (1913-67), British actress

That although artificial teeth are a great blessing, and although a suitable wig may be a charitable covering for a bald head, yet she is committing a sin against her personal appearance as well as against her self-respect if she dyes her hair.
Mary Scharlieb (1845-1930), British gynaecological surgeon, The Seven Ages of Woman, *1915*

BED

The happiest part of a man's life is what he passes lying awake in bed in the morning.
Dr Samuel Johnson (1709-84), English lexicographer, critic and author

The cool kindliness of sheets, that soon smooth away trouble; and the rough male kiss of blankets.
Rupert Brooke (1887-1915), English poet

For I've been born and I've been wed –
all of man's peril comes of bed.
C. H. Webb (1834-1905) American journalist

She isn't a bad bit of goods, the Queen! I wish all the fleas in my bed were as good.
Miguel de Cervantes (1547-1616), Spanish novelist, Don Quixote, *1605*

It is getting too squeaky. The technicians are worried one of the legs might fall off.
BBC Radio Four source, on the bed used in the radio programme The Archers

BEHAVIOUR

If women are supposed to be less rational and more emotional at the beginning of our menstrual cycle when the female hormone is at its lowest level, then why isn't it logical to say that, in those few days, women behave the most like the way men behave all month long?
Gloria Steinem, American writer

The mother-in-law thinks I'm effeminate; not that I mind because, beside her, I am!
Les Dawson, The Les Dawson Joke Book, *1979*

There is a tide in the affairs of women, which, taken at the flood, heads – God knows where.
Lord Byron, *British poet, Don Juan, 1819*

He was the rudest, meanest man I've ever seen. He was terrifically hostile – maybe because he was blind – and everybody hated him but that one secretary he was going to bed with. She was the ugliest thing you've ever seen, but he didn't care because he couldn't see her.
Truman Capote *on James Thurber*

Funny really. When you look at the things that go on these days, my story reads like *Noddy*.
Diana Dors

My candle burns at both ends;
it will not last the night;
But Ah, my foes, and Oh my friends –
It gives a lovely light!
Anon

I'm proud that I was never vulgar. There's no way I'd need a tattoo or dress up in some surgical appliance to give folks a good night out.
Tina Turner, *American singer, referring to Cher*

BIRTH CONTROL

. . . wherefore, since if the parts be smooth, conception is prevented, some anoint that part of the womb on which the seed falls with oil of cedar, or with ointment of lead or with frankincense, commingled with olive oil.
Aristotle *(384-322 BC), Greek philosopher*

The remedy for preventing conception shocks the mind of woman, at the first thought; but prejudice soon flies.
Richard Carlile *(1790-1843), British journalist,* Every Woman's Book; or, What is Love?

If instead of birth control everyone would preach drink control, you would have little poverty, less crime and fewer illegitimate children . . . I speak feelingly; for as my brother Harold John Tennant and I were the last of twelve children, it is more than probable we should never have existed had the fashion of birth control been prevalent in the eighties.
Margot Asquith *(1865-1945),* Places and Persons, *1925*

We want far better reasons for having children than not
knowing how to prevent them.
Dora Russell

The contraceptive pill may reduce the importance of sex
not only as a basis for the division of labour, but as a
guideline in developing talents and interests.
Caroline Bird, American writer, Born Female, 1968

He no play-da-game. He no make-a-da rules!
Earl Butz, American politician, referring to the Pope's stricture
against contraception

Vasectomies and condoms are as safe for women as
anything based on men's behaviour can be.
Spare Rib magazine

Skullion had little use for contraceptives at the best of
times. Unnatural, he called them, and placed them in
the lower social order of things along with elastic-sided
boots and made-up bow ties. Not the sort of attire for a
gentleman.
Tom Sharpe, Porterhouse Blue, 1974

My girlfriend just found out she's been taking aspirins
instead of the pill. Well, at least she doesn't have a
headache – but I do.
Laugh-In, NBC TV, 1969

The pill came to market and changed the sexual and
real estate habits of millions: motel chains were created
to serve them.
Herbert Gold, the New York Times, 1972

Young girl: Have I had any side effects from the pill?
Doctor: Only promiscuity.
Don Orehek, caption in Playboy magazine, 1969

I wonder how he feels, his first game in a Dutch cap.
Barry Davies, commentator, discussing a member of the Holland
football team, 1990 World Cup

Even if a condom in your purse was approaching the
sell-by date, it would still be worth having it.
Ben Elton, British writer and comedian

Some women behave like harlots when they feel the life of a child in their wombs. They induce herbs or other means to cause miscarriage, only to perpetuate their amusement and unchastity. Therefore I shall deprive them from everlasting life and send them to everlasting death.
Bridget of Sweden (1303-73), Swedish nun and visionary,
Revelations *Vol. VII*

The command 'be fruitful and multiply' was promulgated according to our authorities, when the population of the world consisted of two people.
Dean Inge (1860-1954), British churchman, More Lay Thoughts of a Dean, *1931*

Protestant women may take the pill, Roman Catholic women must keep taking the Tablet.
*Irene Thomas, British writer (*The Tablet *is a Roman Catholic newspaper)*

Family Planning – please use rear entrance.
Sign outside the Barnstable Health Centre

Let us have a vast condom within us to protect the health of our soul amid the filth into which it is plunged.
Gustave Flaubert

The unbelieving repulsion on her face was fixed for ever for me like Kean's Macbeth.
John Osborne, writer and playwright, recalling his meeting with Lynn Reid Banks, author of The L-Shaped Room. *(At a rather smart cocktail party, he had offered her a sandwich into which he had inserted a used condom.)*

The best contraceptive is a glass of cold water: not before or after, but instead.
Pakistani delegate at the International Planned Parenthood Conference

It is now quite lawful for a Catholic woman to avoid pregnancy by a resort to mathematics, though she is still forbidden to resort to physics and chemistry.
H. L. Mencken (1880-1956)

Contraceptives should be used on all conceivable occasions.
Spike Milligan, British comedian and writer

I want to tell you a terrific story about oral
contraception. I asked this girl to sleep with me and she
said 'No'.
Woody Allen

If nature had arranged that husbands and wives should
have children alternatively, there would never be more
than three in a family.
Lawrence Housman (1865-1959), English novelist and dramatist

BISEXUALITY

Bisexuality is not so much a cop-out as a fearful
compromise.
Jill Johnston, Lesbian Nation, 1973

I can't understand why more people aren't bisexual. It
would double your chances for a date on Saturday
night.
Woody Allen

BLONDES

Blondes have the hottest kisses. Red-heads are fair-to-
middling torrid, and brunettes are the frigidest of all.
It's something to do with hormones, no doubt.
Ronald Reagan, actor and former American President

Is it possible that blondes also prefer gentlemen?
Mamie Van Doren, American actress, Quote and Unquote, 1970

Who can resist a date with a blonde? She always
wanted me to come back. By God I've been lucky,
haven't I?
*Professor Sir Alan Walters on his appointment as economics
advisor to Margaret Thatcher*

BODY

Really that little dealybob is too far away from the hole.
It should be built right in.
Loretta Lynn, on the female body

Woman has ovaries, a uterus . . . It is often said that she
thinks with her glands. Man superbly ignores the fact
that his anatomy also includes glands, such as the
testicles, and that they secrete hormones.
Simone de Beauvoir (1908-86), French writer

Our [women's] bodies are shaped to bear children and
our lives are a worship out of the processes of creation.
All ambition and intelligence are beside that great
elemental point.
Phyllis McGinley, The Honour of Being a Woman

My bust was visible under the negligee in one scene.
Suddenly, there were Barbra Streisand's breasts and I
was worried that people might concentrate on my body
instead of my acting.
*Barbra Streisand, on seeing rushes of the sex scenes with Nick
Nolte in the film* The Prince of Tides, *1991*

. . . Much like the stump-end of a whist-card pencil.
Dr Marian Greaves, author of The Mastery of Sex Through
Psychology and Religion, *1931, describing the clitoris*

He must have had a magnificent build before his
stomach went in for a career of its own.
Margaret Halsey

When the life of the party wants to express the idea of a
pretty woman in mime, he undulates his two hands in
the air and leers expressively. The notion of a curve is
so closely connected to sexual semantics that some
people cannot resist sniggering at road signs. The most
popular image of the female, despite the exigencies of
the clothing trade, is all boobs and buttocks, a
hallucinating sequence of parabolas and bulges.
Germaine Greer, The Female Eunuch

Like a drawing by a student in a life class who was
sitting at the back without his specs.
Victoria Wood, describing someone's appearance

I would have preferred to omit this chapter, that
women might not become all the more arrogant by
knowing that they also, like men, have testicles, and
that they not only suffer the pain of having to nourish
the child within their bodies . . . but also that they too
put something of their own into it.
I. de Valverde, Spanish anatomist, Historia de la Composicion del
Cuerpo Humano, *1556*

The two women gazed out of the slumped and sagging bodies that had accumulated around them.
Nadine Gordimer, *South African writer and lecturer*, Vital Statistics, *1965*

The womb of a woman is in the number of the insatiable things mentioned in the Scriptures. I cannot tell whether there is anything in the world its greediness may be compared unto; neither hell fire nor the earth being so devouring, as the privy parts of a lascivious woman.
Dr Nicholas de Venette, *quoted in* The Mysteries of Conjugal Love Revealed, *eighteenth century*

Fat is not about lack of self-control or willpower. Fat is about protection, sex nurturance, mothering, strength and assertion. Fat is a social disease.
Susie Orbach, *Feminist psychologist*, Fat is Feminist Issue, *1978*

BOOKS

I didn't know, truly I didn't know. Mine is a life sheltered to the point of stuffiness. I attend no movies, for any motion picture theatre is an enlarged and magnificently decorated lethal chamber to me. I have read but little of Madame Glyn. I did not know that things like *it* were going on. I have misspent my days. When I think of all those hours flung away in reading Henry James and Santayana, when I might have been reading life, throbbing, beating, perfumed life, I practically break down. Where, I ask you, have I been, that no true word of Madame Glyn's literary feats has come to me?
Dorothy Parker, *on Elinor Glyn*, New Yorker, *1927*

Women who love men who hate women who love men too much but love men and on and on . . . you have to feel sorry for the women who buy this stuff and believe it. Even under the best of circumstances men are hard creatures to trap. Women who flatter themselves into thinking they've trapped one are like people who believe they can get rid of the cockroaches in their kitchen. They're in for a big surprise late one night when they turn on the light.
Harry Shearer, *American actor, writer and TV show host, giving his views on 'relationship' books*

A lot of bad novels in which the clitoris is described as
the red pearl and the penis is always described as
engorged and throbbing. Mercy.
*Rita Mae Brown, on being asked about the results of the sexual
revolution*

Is this a book that you would ever wish your wife or
servants to read?
*Mervyn Griffith-Jones at the trial for obscenity of D. H.
Lawrence's novel, Lady Chatterley's Lover*

Sister Susie built her hopes
on the book of Marie Stopes
but I fear from her condition
she must have read the wrong edition.
Madge Kendall

Fair crack of the whip, who reads dictionaries anyway?
You've guessed it, sport – old ladies doing the *Women's
Weekly* crossword and audio-typists who can't spell
'receive'. Correct me if I'm wrong but case in point:

> A red-blooded digger puts the hard word on the
> horny little tart down the local rubbidy . . . she looks
> like she'll come across so he whips her up to his
> brick veneer unit and they're both starkers before the
> froth's gone flat on his Fosters. She's screaming for
> it, so what does this rat-bag do? He sticks his nose
> (wait for it) in a copy of the *Australian Pocket
> Oxford Dictionary*!

Viewed dispassionately thus, I ask you, readers, what
strange minority need does this flaming book meet?
Sir Les Patterson (aka Barry Humphries), Sunday Times, 1977

An interviewer asked me what book I thought best
represented the modern American woman. All I could
think of to answer was: *Madame Bovary.*
*Mary McCarthy (1912-89), American novelist, On the Contrary,
1962*

I'm going to introduce a resolution to have the
Postmaster General stop reading dirty books and deliver
the mail.
Gale McGee

At last an unprintable book that is readable.
*Ezra Pound (1885-1972), American poet, on Henry Miller's
Tropic of Cancer, 1934*

Perversity is the muse of modern literature.
Susan Sontag, *American novelist, critic and screenwriter*

We romantic writers are there to make people feel and
not think. A historical romance is the only kind of book
where chastity really counts.
Barbara Cartland

The modest and chaste woman may be assured that
nothing in here is meant to offend her. Instruction,
upon a matter, of which both men and women are by
far too ignorant, for their welfare and happiness, is the
sole object of this publication. It may shock prejudices,
but it will be approved by reason and due deliberation.
Richard Carlile

BREASTS

It's impossible to be more flat-chested than I am.
Candice Bergen

Uncorsetted, her friendly bust
gives promise of pneumatic bliss.
T. S. Eliot *(1888-1959), American poet and critic*

There are two good reasons why men go to see her. Those are enough.
Howard Hughes (1905-76), *on Jane Russell*

A fine woman shows her charms to most advantage when she seems most to conceal them. The finest bosom in nature is not so fine as imagination forms.
Dr Gregory, A Father's Legacy to His Daughters, *eighteenth century*

It was not a bosom to repose upon, but it was a capital bosom to hang jewels upon.
Charles Dickens (1812-70)

Of course I flaunt my assets. They are big, but I've always had 'em, pushed 'em up, whacked 'em around. Why not make fun when I've earned a fortune with 'em?
Dolly Parton, *actress and singer*

If I hadn't had them, I would have had some made.
Dolly Parton

Even today, every time I open a magazine I get depressed looking at cleavages which look as if they should be offering day trips. If it wasn't for men's infantile obsession with large breasts, women wouldn't experience these humiliating scenarios in the first place.
Jaci Stephen, *columnist*, If Men Had More Up Top We'd Need Less Up Front

Boys, I've got an idea. Let's fill the whole screen with tits.
Hunt Strombert, American film producer, discussing a documentary about the South Seas

I came to London during the seventies with the Three Degrees and was staying at the Hilton Hotel. After a day's shopping, I breezed into reception to collect my key when I noticed a man in front of me staring with his eyes so wide open they were nearly falling out of his head. I thought maybe I knew him, so I said: 'Hello'. When I looked down, I realised the boob tube I was wearing had slipped and I was standing topless in front of a complete stranger.
Sheila Ferguson's *most embarrassing moment*

MORDELL LECTURE, 1978. Professor J. Tits, of the Collège de France, will deliver the Mordell lecture at 5 p.m. on Monday 24th April in the Babbage lecture theatre, New Museums site. The title of the lecture will be 'Rigidity'.
Cambridge University Reporter

Miss World has always had its fair share of knockers.
Julia Morley, organiser of the Miss World Contest

A vacuum with nipples.
Otto Preminger, American film director, on Marilyn Monroe

To read the papers and magazines, you would think we were almost worshipping the female bosom.
Billy Graham, American preacher, 1966

If anything happens to me, please arrange for me to be buried topless.
Mother of actor George Hamilton, after she revealed that, at the age of seventy-three, she had just had her breasts enlarged by silicone implant

BULLSHIT

First, we see how women have been the cause of many troubles, have done great harm to those who govern cities, and have caused in them many divisions ... among the primary causes of the downfall of tyrants, Aristotle puts the injuries they do on account of women, whether rape, violation or the breaking up of marriages.
Nicolò Machiavelli (1469-1527), Italian statesman and writer, Discourses on the First Decade of Livy

The wife is entirely under the power and subjection of her husband.
James Balfour, Scottish judge, The Practiks of Sir James Balfour of Pittendreich, 1550

Woman in her greatest perfection was made to serve and obey man, not to rule and command him.
John Knox (c.1514-72), Scottish religious reformer, First Blast of the Trumpet Against the Monstrous Regiment of Women

How is it that woman, who is soul-less herself, can discern the soul in man? How can she judge about his morality who is herself non-moral? How can she grasp his character when she has no character herself?
Otto Weinger, writer, Sex and Character

It is even possible, quite often, to spot women on the
pill from a certain deadness about their flesh, lustiness
about their eyes and lifelessness in their movements.
Malcolm Muggeridge, British critic, speaking on BBC television,
1965

BUSINESS

I'm forcing more men into my company to get more
sexual tension into the business – because I love the
buzz and the sexuality of verbal foreplay.
Anita Roddick, founder of Body Shop International

My business is a love story with the world.
Luciano Benetton, founder of the Benetton clothing company

Like sex in Victorian England, the reality of Big
Business today is our big dirty secret.
Ralph Nader, American lawyer

I have a tremendous charge out of business. I get the
same sort of feeling that women must have when their
babies pop out.
Sir Terence Conran, British designer, founder of Habitat

I often get invited to boardroom lunches as the token
woman: I find it tempting to say something outrageous.
Jennifer d'Abo, former Chairwoman of Ryman Ltd

A lot of businesses are being started by women who
have been working for idiots for years. They know they
can do their boss's job, but they know they will never
be given it.
Jean Denton, Director of British Nuclear Fuels

If you love your customer to death, you can't go wrong.
Sir Graham Day, Chairman of the Rover Group plc, Cadbury-
Schweppes and Powergen

If there was a good deal or a woman – I would
probably go after the woman.
David Wickens, founder of British Car Auctions and four times
married

I'll tell you what: if you become our Playmate for July,
I'll get you that new addressograph for your
department.
Hugh Hefner, founder of Playboy *magazine, to his subscription
manager, Charlaine Karalus. (After some coaxing, she agreed.)*

I sell projects but I try not to fall in love with them. If
someone says to me, 'I love you', I have more suspicion
of him than the guy who says, 'I just want to make
money', God bless him. He's the guy I want to deal
with.
Adnan Khasoogi

Prince de Joinville: Where? When? How much?
Rachel: Your place, tonight, free.
A business-like exchange of notes from the eighteenth century

Advertising is the most fun you can have with your
clothes on.
*Jerry Della Femina, former advertising executive of Della Femina,
Travisano and Partners*

Don't tell my mother I work in an advertising agency –
she thinks I play piano in a whorehouse.
Jacques Seguela, title of memoirs, 1979

Falling in love with the boss is the cardinal sin in the
office. A girl must look after her boss – be a friend,
public relations officer, colleague and nanny – but never
love him. Nothing is more boring or irritating to his
friends and colleagues than an adoring and possessive
secretary.
Lady Dartmouth

Men will try to use secretaries as status symbols. They
hire them for ornamental reasons. Every time a young
one leaves to get married, they swear they'll go for
someone older and steadier. Then they go right ahead
and hire the next pretty face with 40-40 speeds.
Katherine Whitehorn

Industrial relations are like sexual relations. It's better
between two consenting parties.
Vic Feather (1908-76), British trade union leader, Guardian
Weekly, 1976

Employees make the best dates. You don't have to pick
them up and they're always tax deductible.
Andy Warhol (1928-87), American artist, Exposures, 1979

In a society where people get more or less what they want sexually, it is much more difficult to motivate them in an industrialised context, to make them buy refrigerators and cars.
William S. Burroughs, *American writer, the* Guardian, *1969*

Professionalism, if you like, is not having sex on Thursdays or Fridays.
Don Revie, *British soccer manager, the* Guardian, *1976*

BUTTOCKS

A mystery man on a bicycle is being sought by police following two incidents in which Reading women have been jabbed in the buttocks. The police have been told that a man rode up behind young women in the town, stuck what is believed to be a school compass into them, and rode off.
Quoted in Punch's Country Life *column*

The buttocks are the most aesthetically pleasing part of the body because they are non-functional. Although they conceal an essential orifice, these pointless globes are as near as the human form can ever come to abstract art.
Kenneth Tynan *(1927-80), British journalist and critic*

The essence of life is the smile of round female bottoms, under the shadow of cosmic boredom.
Guy de Maupassant *(1850-93), French novelist*

He kissed the plump mellow yellor smellor melons of her rump, on each plump melonous hemisphere, in their mellow yellow furrow, with obscure prolonged provocative melonsmellonous osculation.
James Joyce *(1882-1941), Irish writer*

How brave a prospect is a broad backside!
Henry Vaughan

Which would you say is my best side, Mr Hitchcock?
Mary Anderson, *actress, posing for photographs for the 1944 film,* Lifeboat

My dear, you're sitting on it.
Alfred Hitchcock *(1899-1980), British-American film director*

It was a stupid compromise.
The explanation of a man with three previous convictions for indecent exposure when he was arrested for baring his buttocks to a group of girls

Buttock fetishism is comparatively rare in our culture
... Girls are often self-conscious about their behinds, draping themselves in long capes and tunics, but it is more often because they are too abundant in that region than otherwise.
Germaine Greer, The Female Eunuch

George Moore unexpectedly pinched my behind. I felt rather honoured that my behind should have drawn the attention of the great master of English prose.
Ilka Chase, *American actress and author*

CAREER

A caress is better than a career.
Elizabeth Marbury *(1856-1933), American playwright*, Careers for Women, *1933*

CAUTION

Beware of men on aeroplanes. The minute a man reaches 30,000 feet, he immediately becomes consumed by distasteful sexual fantasies which involve doing uncomfortable things in those tiny toilets. These men should not be encouraged; their fantasies are sadly low-rent and unimaginative. Affect an aloof, cool demeanour as soon as any man tries to draw you out. Unless, of course, he's the pilot.
Cynthia Heimel

Woe to the man who tries to be frank in love-making.
George Sand *(Armandine Lucille Dupin, 1804-76), French writer*

Anger repressed can poison a relationship as surely as the cruelest words.
Joyce Brothers, *American psychologist and journalist, 1922*

Among external causes are springtime, which is a
particularly dangerous season, warm climates, improper
clothes, rich food, indigestion, mental overwork,
nervousness, habits of defective cleanliness, especially of
the local kind, prolonged sitting or standing, too
monotonous walking, sitting cross-legged, spanking,
late rising, petting and indulgence corsets that produce
stagnation or hyperaemia of blood and great straining
of memory.
Professor Hall, talking about lust

You are throwing away the seed that has been handed
down to you as a trust instead of keeping it and
ripening it for bringing a son to you later.
*Lord Baden-Powell, founder of the Boy Scout movement, giving
advice to boys*

CENSORSHIP

The British Board of Censors will not pass any
seduction scene unless the seducer has one foot on the
floor. Apparently sex in England is something like
snooker.
Fred Allen

If a man is pictured chopping off a woman's breast, it
only gets an 'R' rating; but if, God forbid, a man is
pictured kissing a woman's breast, it gets an 'X' rating.
Why is violence more acceptable than tenderness?
Sally Struthers, quoted in Life *magazine, 1984*

Censorship feeds the dirty mind more than the four-
letter word itself.
Dick Cavett, American talk-show host, quoted in Playboy
magazine, 1971

It is appalling that naked women cannot be kept out of
the nation's living-room.
Billy Graham, American preacher, backing censorship

I've got nothing against sex, it's a marvellous human
activity; but it was watching others do it all the time
that got me down.
*John Trevelyan, British film censor, explaining why he resigned,
1974*

That must be removed.

Margaret Thatcher when Chairwoman of the Finchley Arts Society, in the mid-1960s. (Making a surprise visit to one of their exhibitions, she walked straight past various outrageous exhibits, including a sculpture constructed out of condoms, and stood before a canvas with a single white splash on it. When the puzzled organisers asked why this innocent picture offended, she explained that the canvas clearly portrayed a male orgasm.)

The steamy film *9½ Weeks* has been temporarily banned from Worthing's Dome cinema until it has been privately viewed by Worthing's council's moral watchdogs. The film *Body Lust*, the best bit of crumpet in Denmark, will be shown instead.

Reported in the Worthing Guardian

Censorship, like charity, should begin at home; but unlike charity it should end there.

Clare Boothe Luce *(1903-87), American journalist, diplomat, politician and playwright*

C H A N G E

A century and a half ago they wore no knickers and girls read the Bible; now they wear impenetrable body-stockings and read *Portnoy's Complaint*.

Kenneth Tynan

I don't think he has changed that much. He still eyes a pretty lady – and why not? This is part of his magnetism. This is Warren. What has changed, I hope, is that he doesn't seem to have that urge to bed these lovely ladies. Now that's a major change.

Annette Bening, *on being asked what convinced her that marriage had changed Warren Beatty*

We're living in an age where you have to call a chick and ask her if she'll wear a dress tonight. And they say: You're weird.

Tim Rose

It's hard for me to get used to these changing times. I can remember when the air was clean and the sex was dirty.

George Burns, *American actor and comedian*

We were born in an era in which it was a disgrace for
women to be sexually responsible. We matured in an
era in which it was an obligation.
Janet Harris, American writer, The Prime of Ms. America, *1975*

C H A R M

'Charm' – which means the power to effect work
without employing brute force – is indispensable to
women. Charm is a woman's strength just as strength is
a man's charm.
Havelock Ellis (1859-1939), British psychologist and author

It's a sort of bloom on a woman. If you have it, you
don't need to have anything else; and if you don't have
it, it doesn't much matter what else you have.
J. M. Barrie (1860-1937), British playwright

Charming women can true converts make
We love the precepts for the teacher's sake.
George Farquhar (1678-1707)

She lacks the indefinable charm of weakness.
Oscar Wilde

Men get to be a mixture of the charming mannerisms of
the women they have known.
F. Scott Fitzgerald (1896-1940), American novelist

You know what charm is: a way of getting the answer
yes without having asked any clear questions.
Albert Camus (1913-62), French writer

C H A S T I T Y

Lord, give me chastity – but not yet.
Saint Augustine (354-430)

As a child of eight, Mr Trout had once kissed a girl of
six under the mistletoe at a Christmas party, but there
his sex life has come to an abrupt halt.
P. G. Wodehouse (1881-1975), British humorist and novelist,
Bachelors Anonymous, *1973*

Of all sexual aberrations, perhaps the most peculiar is
chastity.
Remy de Gourmont (1858-1915), French critic and novelist

A woman's chastity consists, like an onion, of a series of coats.
Nathaniel Hawthorne *(1804-64), American novelist*

An unattempted woman cannot boast of her chastity.
Michel de Montaigne *(1533-92), French essayist*

In the old days poverty kept Latin women chaste: hard work, too little sleep, these were the things that saved their humble homes from corruption.
Juvenal *(60-130 AD), Roman satirist*

Only one woman in thousands has been endowed with the God-given aptitude to live in chastity and virginity ... God fashioned her body so that she could be with a man, to have and to rear children. No woman should be ashamed of that which God made and intended her.
Martin Luther *(1483-1546), German Protestant reformer*

Nothing makes women more esteemed by the opposite sex than chastity; whether it be that we always prize most those who are hardest to come at, or that nothing beside chastity, with its collateral attendants, truth, fidelity and constancy, gives the man a property in the person he loves, and consequently endears her to him above all things.
Anon, Spectator, 1711

She is chaste who nobody has asked.
Ovid *(43-17 BC), Roman poet*

The common man believes that in order to be chaste, a woman must not be too clever; in truth it is doing chastity too little honour to believe it can be found beautiful only by the blind.
Marie de Jars *(1565-1645), French writer, Proumenoir, 1594*

CHASTITY BELT

There is no doubt that the practice is a means of suppressing and controlling the sexual behaviour of women. Female circumcision is a physiological chastity belt.
Sue Armstrong, *South African journalist*

The advantages are manifold. Not only will the purity of the virgin be maintained but the fidelity of the wife exacted. The husband will leave the wife without fear that his honour will be outraged and his affections estranged.

A French merchandising house advertising a chastity belt. The Girdle of Chastity *(Eric Dingwall), 1880*

. . . Made of iron, and consisting of a belt and a piece which came up under and was locked in position, so neatly made that once a woman was bridled it was out of the question for her to indulge in the gentle pleasure, as there were only a few little holes for her to piss through.

Pierre de Bourdeille, Seigneur de Brantome *(c.1540-1614), French writer, describing the chastity belt,* The Lives of Gallant Ladies, *sixteenth century*

The Crusaders, we are told, put their wives into chastity belts before they sailed off for the Holy Land. They did not, for certain, put their own sexual equipment out of action for the duration.

Mary Stott

C H I L D B I R T H

None of the fifteen legal men, comprising judge, senior and junior barristers and solicitors, had ever witnessed childbirth. Is it possible, the judge was to ask, for a woman to give birth standing up? Women have given birth underwater, in aeroplanes, in comas, lying unnaturally flat on their backs in hospital beds and even after death, but this man wondered if they could do it standing up . . .

Nell McCafferty

Somewhere on this globe, every ten seconds, there is a woman giving birth to a child. She must be found and stopped.

Sam Levenson *(1911-80)*

Simpson succeeded in proving that there was no harm in giving anaesthetics to men, because God put Adam into a deep sleep when he extracted his rib. But male ecclesiastics remained unconvinced as regards the sufferings of women, at any rate in childbirth.

Bertrand Russell *(1872-1970), British philosopher*

My obstetrician was so dumb that when I gave birth he forgot to cut the cord. For a year that kid followed me everywhere. It was like having a dog on a leash.
Joan Rivers, American comedienne

To enter life by way of the vagina is as good a way as any.
Henry Miller (1891-1980), American novelist

I have an intense desire to return to the womb. Anybody's.
Woody Allen

To my embarrassment, I was born in bed with a lady.
Wilson Mizner (1876-1933)

If men had to have babies they would only ever have one each.
Diana, Princess of Wales

Often women have babies because they can't think of anything better to do.
Lord Beaumont of Whitley, British prelate, politician and journalist

I had a Jewish delivery: they knock you out with the first pain: they wake you up when the hairdresser shows.
Joan Rivers

Dr Snow gave that blessed chloroform and the effect was soothing, quieting and delightful beyond measure.
Queen Victoria (1819-1901), describes her labour in her journal of 1853

Publication is the male equivalent of childbirth.
Richard Ackland, British politician and writer, 1974

The artificial insemination of animals is taken for granted to improve the breed and product. Human insemination is a different ball-game.
The Catholic Register of Canada

Dear Mary, we all knew you had it in you.
Dorothy Parker's telegram congratulating a friend on the successful outcome of her pregnancy, 1915

CHILDREN

Sometimes when I look at my children I say to myself,
'Lilian, you should have stayed a virgin'.
Lilian Carter, mother of former American President Jimmy Carter

An ugly baby is a very nasty object, and the prettiest is
frightful when undressed.
Queen Victoria

It takes a woman twenty years to make a man of her
son, and another woman twenty minutes to make a fool
of him.
Helen Rowland

A loud noise at one end and no sense of responsibility at
the other.
Father Ronald Knox (1888-1957), British clergyman and writer

From the moment of birth, when the Stone-Age baby
confronts the twentieth-century mother, the baby is
subjected to these forces of violence called love, as its
father and mother and their parents and their parents
before them, have been. These forces are mainly
concerned with destroying most of its potential.
R. D. Laing (1927-89), British psychiatrist

Babies are the enemies of the human race.
Isaac Asimov, American author

Don't take up a man's time talking about the smartness
of your children; he wants to talk to you about the
smartness of his.
Ed (E. W.) Howe (1853-1937), American journalist and novelist

Before I got married I had six theories about bringing
up children; now I have six children, and no theories.
John Wilmot, Earl of Rochester (1647-80), English poet

Men are generally more careful of the breed of their
horses and dogs than of their children.
*William Penn (1644-1718), religious leader and founder of the
state of Pennsylvania*

I learned to walk as a baby, and I haven't had a lesson
since.
Marilyn Monroe, on being asked about her famous wiggle

Oh my son's my son till he gets him a wife,
but my daughter's my daughter all her life.
Dinah Mulock Craik (1826-87), *British writer and poet*, Young
and Old, c.1887

CHIVALRY

Remember, men, we're fighting for this woman's
honour, which is probably more than she ever did.
Groucho Marx, *American comedian*, Duck Soup, 1933

Every man I meet wants to protect me. I can't figure out
what from.
Mae West (1892-1980), *American actress*

CLASS

There is no middle-class sexual style for men. What
would it be based on? Golfing? Discussing stock
options? Attending church? Downing highballs?
Edmund White, *American writer, 1979*

COMMUNICATION

Whereas a lot of men used to ask for conversation when
they really wanted sex, nowadays they often feel
obliged to ask for sex even when they really want
conversation.
Katherine Whitehorn, *British journalist*

I try to talk to one person. I've got this picture of a
woman, a housewife, young or young at heart. She's
probably on her own virtually all day. She's bored with
the routine of housework and her own company, and
just for her I'm the chatty, slightly cheeky romantic
visitor.
David Hamilton, *British disc jockey, quoted in* Is This Your Life?
Images of Women In the Media *(ed. J. King and Mary Stott, 1977)*

COMPLIMENTS

There are only two superlative compliments you can
receive from a woman: 'I think you're a master chef,
and I think you're a good lay.' The two basic drives in
life.
Rod Steiger, *American actor*

Women are never disarmed by compliments. Men always are. That is the difference between the sexes.
Oscar Wilde, An Ideal Husband

The Queen did fish for men's souls, and had so sweet a bait that no one could escape her network.
Christopher Hatton, on Queen Elizabeth I

C O S M I C

Amazing! Astonishing! Still can't get over the fantastic idea that when you're looking at a girl, you are looking at somebody who is guaranteed to have on her – a cunt! They all have cunts! Right under their dresses! Cunts for fucking!
Philip Roth, American novelist, Portnoy's Complaint, 1969

The sex organ has a poetic power, like a comet.
Joan Miró (1893-1983), Spanish artist

I have been led to imagine that the few extraordinary women who have rushed in eccentrical directions out of the orbit prescribed to their sex were male spirits, confined by mistake in female frames.
Mary Wollstonecraft (1759-97), British writer, A Vindication of the Rights of Woman, 1792

One may see a girl in her mother-nakedness dancing around a hippy guy, and another looking at the spectacle with passing amusement. Her boobs and the hirsute 'pelvic triangle' look prominent in the soliciting gestures.
Som Deva, writer, The Marching Eros, describing the sexual habits of the alternative society

The underground was rather shy and inhibited. Later, though, when 'horizontal recruitment' became the more favoured form of recruitment on the libbo left, then it really did get going. The libertarian loony left scene of the early '70s was very strong on rogering and leg-over: it was a leg-over-based scene.
David Robins, writer and commentator, dicussing sex in the 1960s

C R E A T I V I T Y

We don't call it sin today – we call it self-expression.
Baroness Stocks, British politician

In a non-permissive age, she made remarkable inroads against the taboos of her day, and did so without even lowering her neckline.
Leslie Halliwell, *British journalist and author*

The fanny lap your patter up
they like when you're rough
and if you dinnae fuck them
there's other bits of stuff.
We take them to the bar
and get them steaming first
and if you dinnae get a bag off
you can always steal their purse.
Dave Robertson, *poet*, I'm a Gadgie

CRITICS

Western man, especially the Western critic, still finds it very hard to go into print and say: 'I recommend you go and see this because it gave me an erection.'
Kenneth Tynan *in* Playboy *magazine, 1977*

It is better to be thought of as a heart-throb than as a pig.
Tom Conti, *actor*

DATING

I took a gentleman on a beautiful trail ride. He wasn't a good rider so I put him on the safest, slowest horse in the barn. As luck would have it, his horse stepped in a hornet's nest. After that episode, in which his horse ran faster than Secretariat, ardour hit the deep freeze. My second-worst date occurred when a quite pretty lady asked me out and I was thrilled that she had noticed me. I met her at the appointed time at a posh restaurant only to be greeted by her and her husband. I was both naïve and shocked.
Rita Mae Brown, *American writer*

Men generally pay for all expenses on a date . . . either sex, however, may bring a little gift, its value to be determined by the bizarreness of the sexual request to be made later that evening.
P. J. O'Rourke, *Modern Manners, 1983*

Anything my mother had anything to do with goes in
the 'worst' category. But the very worst was when my
sister was at the University of Wisconsin and I was a
teenager and my girlfriend and I came to visit her for
the weekend and she fixed us up with two of her
discards, in my case a very tall gentleman named
'Moose'.
Alice Kahn

It's terrific if you're a computer.
Rita Mae Brown *on being asked what she thought about
computer dating*

Dates used to be made days or even weeks in advance.
Now dates tend to be made the day after. That is, you
get a phone call from someone who says, 'If anyone
asks, I was out to dinner with you last night, okay?'
P. J. O'Rourke, Modern Manners, *1983*

A date, at this juncture in history, is any pre-arranged
meeting with a member of the opposite sex towards
whom you have indecent intentions . . . One does not
have to sleep with, or even touch, someone who has
paid for your meal. All those obligations are hereby
rendered null and void, and any man who doesn't think
so needs a quick jab in the kidney.
Cynthia Heimel, *American writer*, Sex Tips for Girls, *1983*

While at Cambridge, a friend of mine – a friend, you
understand – had been fixed up with a blind date. Being
an optimist, he called at a chemist on the afternoon of
the big day and bought himself a packet of
contraceptives. That evening he met his date. He
recognised her. She had sold him the contraceptives.
Tim Brooke-Taylor, *writer and member of 'The Goodies'*

DEPRAVITY

The mother complained that her son, an only child, was
becoming truculent, had started smoking, had been seen
entering a public house and was keeping company with
a girl. Inspector McCann began to investigate. 'I found
that the son was 36,' he stated.
The Birmingham Post

At both services in the morning, it is intended to preach
a series of sermons on the 'deadly sins', omitting lust.
Our Church Review

Beware of veneryous acts before the first sleep, and
specially beware of such things after dinner or after a
full stomach, for it doth engender the cramp and the
gout and other displeasures.
Andrew Borde, Compendyous Regyment of A Dyetary of Health,
sixteenth century

I believe in the total depravity of inanimate things . . .
the elusiveness of soap, the knottiness of strings, the
transitory nature of buttons, the inclination of
suspenders to twist and of hooks to forsake their lawful
eyes and cleave only unto the hairs of their hapless
owner's head.
Katherine Ashley (1840-1916)

D E S I R E

Where they love they do not desire and where they
desire they do not love.
Sigmund Freud (1865-1939), Austrian psychiatrist

The man's desire is for the woman; the woman's desire
is for the desire of the man.
Samuel Taylor Coleridge (1772-1834), English poet

Those who restrain desire, do so because theirs is weak
enough to be restrained.
William Blake (1757-1827), British poet and painter, The
Marriage of Heaven and Hell, *1793*

Some desire is necessary to keep life in motion.
Dr Samuel Johnson

I have to find a girl attractive or it's like trying to start a
car without an ignition key.
Jonathan Aitken, British politician, 1979

Ever since my childhood I have been accustomed to see
the face of every man who has passed me light up with
desire. Many women will be disgusted to hear that I
have always taken this as homage. Is it despicable to be
the flower whose perfume people long to inhale, the
fruit they long to taste?
Caroline (La Belle) Otero (1868-1965), actress

It is a barbarous custom that forbids the maid to make advances in love, or that confines these advances to the eye, the fingers, the gesture, the motion, the manner . . . And now let us examine the carnal desires of the body itself, whence has arisen unconscionable harm to human life. Justly may we say with Cato of Utica: if the world could be rid of women, we should not be without God in our intercourse. For truly without the wickedness of women, to say nothing of witchcraft, the world would remain proof against innumerable dangers.
Heinrich Dramer and **Jakob Sprenger**, *German Dominican monks*, Malleus Maleficarum: The Classic Study of Witchcraft, 1456

Want is the mistress of invention.
Sussanna Centlivre *(1667-1723)*

He wondered why sexual shyness, which excites the desire of dissolute women, arouses the contempt of decent ones.
Colette *(1873-1954), French novelist*, Armande, 1944

I write to be sexually desirable.
Kenneth Tynan *to his wife*

DIFFERENCES

Men are generally more law-abiding than women. Women have the feeling that since they didn't make the rules, the rules have nothing to do with them.
Diane Johnson

The main difference between men and women is that men are lunatics and women are idiots.
Dame Rebecca West *(1892-1983), British novelist and journalist*

God made men stronger but not necessarily more intelligent. He gave women intuition and femininity. And, used properly, that combination easily jumbles the brain of any man I've ever met.
Farrah Fawcett, *American actress*

Women represent the triumph of matter over mind: men represent the triumph of mind over morals.
Oscar Wilde, The Picture of Dorian Gray, 1891

Men always want to be a woman's first love. We
women have a more subtle intent about things. What
we like is to be a man's first romance.
Oscar Wilde, A Woman of No Importance

Women are not men's equals in anything except
responsibility.
We are not their inferiors either, or even their superiors.
We are quite simply different races.
Phyllis McGinley, American poet

The reason husbands and wives do not understand each
other is because they belong to different sexes.
Dorothy Dix (1870-1951), American journalist

I believe in the difference between men and women. In
fact, I embrace the difference.
Elizabeth Taylor

Mr Darwin . . . has failed to hold definitely before his
mind the principle that the difference of sex, whatever it
may consist in, must itself be subject to natural selection
and to evolution.
Antoinette Brown Blackwell (1825-1921), American feminist
writer, The Sexes Throughout Nature

The little rift between the sexes is astonishingly widened
by simply teaching one set of catchwords to the girls
and another to the boys.
Robert Louis Stevenson (1850-94), Scottish novelist and poet

Man's love is of man's life a thing apart, 'Tis woman's
whole existence.
Lord Byron (1788-1824), British poet, Don Juan

Semen maketh man . . . sex merely expresses the totality
of differences between male and female.
Sir Solly Zuckerman, British scientist

For him she is sex – absolute sex, no less. She is defined
and differentiated with reference to man and not he
with reference to her; she is the incidental, the
unessential as opposed to the essential. He is the
subject, he is the absolute – she is the other.
Simone de Beauvoir (1908-86), French writer, The Second Sex

When a man goes on a date he wonders if he is going to
get lucky. A woman already knows.
Frederike Ryder

DISEASE

President Amin of Uganda in his capacity as his country's Health Minister, has nicknamed venereal disease 'Good Hope' so that sufferers will not be embarrassed when seeing a doctor.
Report in the Daily Telegraph

. . .Viv Richards is giving Patrick Patterson the clap.
Richie Benaud, *sports comentator, when the West Indies cricket captain tried to attract a player's attention*

DIVORCE

The difference between divorce and legal separation is that a legal separation gives a husband time to hide his money.
Johnny Carson

When a couple decide to divorce, they should inform both sets of parents before having a party and telling all their friends. This is not only courteous but practical. Parents may be very willing to pitch in with comments, criticism and malicious gossip of their own to help the divorce along.
P. J. O'Rourke

You never really know a man until you've divorced him.
Zsa Zsa Gabor

Divorce is the sacrament of adultery.
French proverb

What scares me about divorce is that my children might put me in a home for unwed mothers.
Teressa Skelton

Getting divorced just because you don't love a man is almost as silly as getting married just because you do.
Zsa Zsa Gabor

Fission after fusion.
Rita Mae Brown

Remarriage is an excellent test of just how amicable your divorce was.
Margo Kaufman

In our family we don't divorce our men – we bury
them.
Ruth Gordon

It is he who has broken the bond of marriage – not I. I
only break its bondage.
Oscar Wilde

My husband and I will soon be celebrating our Golden
Anniversary of cloudless separation.
*Madame Aubernon, French hostess, commenting on her husband
who left her after only a few days of marriage*

A Roman divorced from his wife was highly blamed by
his friends, who demanded, 'Was she not chaste? Was
she not fair? Was she not faithful?' Holding out his
shoe, he asked them whether it was not new and well
made. 'Yet,' added he, 'None of you can tell where it
pinches me.'
Plutarch (46-120), Greek philosopher and biographer

Caesar's wife must be above suspicion.
Julius Caesar (100-44BC), Roman general and statesman

Should a husband be or become of so cold a nature as
to be unable to have carnal relations with his wife of the
sort proper between husband and wife, then the prelate
grants perpetual divorce to the couple and the woman
may remarry according to her will and pleasure.
*Jean Boutillier, French jurist, referring to divorce laws in France,
fourteenth century*

So many persons think divorce a panacea for every ill,
who find out, when they try it, that the remedy is worse
than the disease.
Dorothy Dix (1861-1951), American journalist, Dorothy Dix, Her
Book, *1926*

Judge: You want a divorce on the grounds that your
husband is rather careless about his appearance.
Woman: Yes, Your Honour – he hasn't made one for
three years.
Anon

Being divorced is like being hit by a Mack truck. If you
live through it, you start looking very carefully to the
right and to the left.
Jean Kerr, Mary, Mary, *1960*

If divorce has increased one thousand per cent, don't
blame the women's movement. Blame our obsolete sex
roles on which our marriages were based.
Betty Friedan, American writer

D O M I N A T I O N

In losing a husband, one loses a master who is often an
obstacle to the enjoyment of many things.
Madeleine de Scudery (1607-1701), French novelist and poet

I have no wish for a second husband. I had enough of
the first. I like to have my own way – to lie down
mistress, and get up master.
Susanna Moodie (1803-85), Canadian writer and poet, Roughing
it in the Bush, *1852*

D R E S S

To attract men, women should dress glamorously in a
low cut dress or short skirt.
Miss Whiplash (aka Lindi St Clair)

A witch and a bitch always dress up for each other,
because otherwise the witch would upstage the bitch, or
the bitch would upstage the witch, and the result would
be havoc.
Tennessee Williams (1911-83), American playwright

Women dress alike all over the world; they dress to be
annoying to other women.
Elsa Schiaparelli (1896-1973), Italian designer

Most women dress as if they had been a mouse in a
previous incarnation, or hope to be one in the next.
Edith Sitwell (1887-1964), English poet

The prettiest dresses are worn to be taken off.
*Jean Cocteau (1891-1963), French writer, painter and film
director*

As an article of dress for the girl, the corset must be
looked upon as distinctly prejudicial to health, and as
entirely unnecessary.
Howard A. Kelly, American gynaecologist, Medical Gynaecology,
1909

There is no such thing as a moral dress – it's people who are moral or immoral.
Jennie Jerome Churchill (1854-1921), British hostess, editor and playwright

An after-dinner speech should be like a lady's dress - long enough to cover the subject and short enough to be interesting.
R. A. 'Rab' Butler (1902-82), British Conservative politician

This ad makes me look better than I thought possible.
Nadia Comaneci, Olympic gold medal gymnast, on her new career modelling underwear

Not only did she wear short tunics, but she dressed herself in tabards and garments open at the sides, besides the matter is notorious since when she was captured she was wearing a surcoat cloak of gold, open on all sides, a cap on her head, and her hair cropped round in man's style. And in general, having cast aside all womanly decency, not only to the scorn of feminine modesty, but also of well-instructed men, she had worn the apparel and garments of most dissolute men, and, in addition, had some weapons of defence.
One of the charges made against Joan of Arc at her trial, quoted in The Trial of Jeanne d'Arc *by W. P. Barrett, 1431*

The Republican Party couldn't make up their minds whether I'd be mistaken for a trollop or for the Queen of England. But silly as the request was, I stopped wearing purple.
Elizabeth Taylor (when married to John Warner, a politician) on being told by a delegation from the Republican Party that she could no longer wear purple

All women's dresses are merely variations on the eternal struggle between admitted desire to dress and the unadmitted desire to undress.
Lin Yutang (1895-1976), Chinese writer

You don't have to signal a social conscience by looking like a frump. Lace knickers won't hasten the holocaust, you can ban the bomb in a feather boa just as well as without, and a mild interest in the length of hemlines doesn't necessarily disqualify you from reading *Das Kapital* and agreeing with every word.
Elizabeth Bibesco (1897-1945), British author

I dress for women and undress for men.
Angie Dickinson

You'd be surprised how much it costs to look this cheap.
Dolly Parton

It is difficult to see why lace is so expensive; it is mostly holes.
Mary Wilson Little

Brevity is the soul of lingerie.
Dorothy Parker (1893-1967), American writer and journalist

I only put clothes on so that I'm not naked when I go out shopping.
Julia Roberts, American actress

DRINK

One more drink and I'll be under the host.
Dorothy Parker

It provokes the desire, but it takes away the performance. Therefore much drink may be said to be an equivocator with lechery.
Porter in Shakespeare's Macbeth

A man who exposes himself when he is intoxicated has not the art of getting drunk.
Dr Samuel Johnson

Alcohol is like love: the first kiss is magic, the second is intimate, the third is routine. After that you just take the girl's clothes off.
Raymond Chandler (1888-1959), American novelist

A fuddled woman is a shameful sight, a prey to anyone, and serve her right.
Ovid (43BC-17AD), Roman poet

All along the line, physically, mentally, morally, alcohol is a weakening and deadening force, and it is worth a great deal to save women and girls from its influence.
Beatrice Potter Webb (1858-1943), British writer and social reformer

Alcohol was a threat to women, for it released men from the moral control they had learned from a diet of preaching and scolding from ministers and mothers alike.
Alice Rossi, American educator, scholar and editor, The Feminist Papers, 1973

Nothing equals the joy of the drinker, except the joy of the wine in being drunk.
French saying

No poems can please for long or live that are written by water-drinkers.
Horace (65-8BC), Roman poet and satirist

A mind of the calibre of mine cannot derive its nutriment from cows.
George Bernard Shaw

I may not here omit those two main plagues, and common dotages of humankind, wine and women, which have infatuated and besotted myriads of people. They go commonly together.
Robert Burton (1577-1640), English philosopher

Wine gives a man nothing . . . it only puts in motion what had been locked up in frost.
Dr Samuel Johnson

Wine makes a man better pleased with himself; I do not say that it makes him more pleasing to others.
Dr Samuel Johnson

Isadora Duncan probably represents the maximum possible development of emotion at the expense of intellect. She was a creature of impulse and the impulses were usually bad ones. She drank champagne as a thirsty horse drinks water.
London's Weekly, 1933

EMOTION

It's scary . . . so personal, giving people the opportunity to see if I'm a good kisser or not. You see, I'm not into sex for the sake of it. I think love scenes are more powerful if it's about communication between two people. It's not about sucking face, it's about emotion.
Patrick Swayze, American actor

All the little hoops were set up for me to jump through, and when you jump, you get a reward – an image. But it's the image they supply . . . You become a perfect couple, or the faded English rose, or the wronged woman, or the rock 'n' roll slut, or whatever. It has very little to do with real, manageable emotions.
Marianne Faithfull, British singer and actress, referring to her relationship with Mick Jagger in City Limits *magazine, 1981*

E Q U A L I T Y

It is naïve in the extreme for women to expect to be regarded as equals by men . . . so long as they persist in a subhuman (i.e. animal-like) behaviour during sexual intercourse. I'm referring . . . to the outlandish PANTING, GASPING, MOANING, SOBBING, WRITHING, SCRATCHING, BITING, SCREAMING, and the seemingly invariable OH MY GOD . . . all so predictably integral to pre-, post-, and orgasmic stages of intercourse.
Terry Southern

Whatever women do they must do twice as well as men to be thought half as good. Luckily, this is not difficult.
Charlotte Whitton (1896-1975), the former Mayor of Ottowa

It's time people stood up and said women are getting too much of the action.
Businesswoman Tina Knight, who insists on no-pregnancy agreements with new recruits

Men seldom make passes at a girl who surpasses.
Franklin P. Jones

Once made equal to a man, woman becomes his superior.
Socrates (c. 469-399BC), Greek philosopher

I refuse to consign the whole male sex to the nursery. I insist on believing that some men are my equals.
Brigid Brophy, British writer

Women who want to be equal to men lack ambition.
Anon

You're used. Used by what you are, eat, believe and
who you sleep with. You can't stop it. If you want
equality it has to start in bed. If he won't give it to you
there, rip him off.
Jane Gallion

There will never be complete equality until women
themselves help to make laws and elect lawmakers.
Susan B. Anthony (1820-1906), The Arena, *1897*

All this pitting of sex against sex, of quality against
quality; all this claiming of superiority and imputing of
inferiority belong to the private-school stage of human
existence where there are sides, and it is necessary for
one side to beat another side.
Virginia Woolf (1882-1941), British novelist and critic, A Room
of One's Own, *1929*

A career woman who has survived the hurdle of
marriage and maternity encounters a new obstacle: the
hostility of men.
Caroline Bird, American writer, Born Female, *1968*

There are very few jobs that actually require a penis or
vagina. All other jobs should be open to everybody.
Florynce R. Kennedy, American lawyer and civil rights activist,
1974

I'm not a believer in equality and my attitude is that
women are supposed to be pretty and nice. A woman
should be a woman.
Jim Davidson, British comedian, 1986

The real theatre of the sex war is the domestic hearth.
Germaine Greer

EROTICISM

[He] twisted my nipples as though tuning a radio.
Lisa Alther, American novelist, Kinflicks, *1976*

She has been described as the Maharani of Malice, the
Empress of Erotica, the Princess of Pulp, the Pasha of
Porn. Despite having received the most spectacularly
worst reviews ever written in India, she is the country's
bestselling writer.
The Sunday Times Magazine, *on Indian author Shobhan De*

This lady is a very dirty lady. Her books are full of
wicked and filthy thoughts.
Mr Sanjay Aggarwal on Shobhan De

I am reading everything she is writing. In one book I am
counting seventy-three copulations. I am shocked only.
Really – her head is full of perversions.
*Mr Satish Lal (who makes carbuncle grinders in Bangalore) on
Shobhan De*

He moved his lips about her ears and neck as though in
thirsting search of an erogenous zone. A waste of time,
he knew from experience. Erogenous zones were either
everywhere or nowhere.
Joseph Heller, American novelist, Good as Gold, 1979

My pictures are not just blatant full-frontals, they are
very tasteful. But they tried to insist that women just
wanted full-frontal dangly bits.
*Nikki Downey, For Women photographer and ex-Penthouse
model*

There is no difference.
*Pablo Picasso (1881-1973), Spanish painter and sculptor, when
asked what was the difference between art and eroticism*

The residue of virility in the woman's organism is
utilised by nature in order to eroticise her: otherwise the
functioning of the maternal apparatus would wholly
submerge her in the painful tasks of reproduction and
motherhood.
*Marie Bonaparte (1882-1962), French psychoanalyst, sexologist
and educator*

Women have been complaining to us for years that
there is nothing like this on the market. They have a
right to look at erotic pictures of beautiful men. They
want explicit articles about sex. After all, men have
been open and free about their sexuality for a long time.
Isabel Koprowski, *the former editor of* Forum, *on the launch of*
For Women *magazine*

Colette wrote of vegetables as if they were love objects
and of sex as if it were an especially delightful
department of gardening.
Brigid Brophy, *British writer*, 1000 Makers of the 20th Century

EXCESS

Too much of a good thing can be wonderful.
Mae West

I have never been afraid of excess. Excess on occasion is
exhilarating. It prevents moderation from acquiring the
deadening effect of a habit.
W. Somerset Maugham, The Summing Up, *1938*

Moderation is a fatal thing. Nothing succeeds like
excess.
Oscar Wilde, A Woman of No Importance, *1893*

EXPERIENCE

Experience is a good teacher, but her fees are very high.
W. R. Inge *(1860-1954), Dean of St Paul's, London*

You should make a point of trying every experience
once – except incest and folk-dancing.
Arnold Bax, *quoted in the* Scotsman

FAMILY

The fact of the matter is that the prime responsibility of
a woman probably is to be on earth long enough to find
the best mate possible for herself, and conceive children
who will improve the species.
Norman Mailer, *American writer*, The Presidential Papers, *1963*

I have a wife, I have sons: all of them hostages given to
fate.
Lucan *(39-65AD), Roman poet*

What a marvellous place to drop one's mother-in-law!
Marshal Ferdinand Foch *(1851-1929), French soldier, on visiting
the Grand Canyon*

He that hath wife and children hath given hostages to
fortune, for they are impediments to great enterprises,
either of virtue or mischief.
Francis Bacon *(1561-1626), English philosopher,* Of Marriage
and Single Life, *1597*

FANTASY

The times being what they were, if she hadn't existed
we would have had to invent her, and we did, in a way.
She was the Fifties' fiction, the lie that women has no
sexual needs, that she is there to cater to or enhance a
man's needs.
Molly Haskell, *on women in male fantasies,* From Reverence to
Rape

And the crazy part of it was even if you were clever,
even if you spent your adolescence reading John Donne
and Shaw, even if you studied history or zoology or
physics and hoped to spend your life pursuing some
difficult and challenging career, you still had a mind full
of all the soupy longings that every high-school girl was
awash in . . . underneath it, all you longed to be was
annihilated by love, to be swept of your feet, to be filled
up by a giant prick spouting sperm, soapsuds, silk and
satins and, of course, money.
Erica Jong

She is every man's fantasy mistress. She gave you the
impression that, if your imagination had to sin, it could
at least be congratulated on its impeccable taste.
Alistair Cooke, *British journalist*

She has made forty films, attempted suicide at least
twice, married three men and has shared passion with
many more. Her rampant sexuality made her a fantasy
figure for men.
The TV Times *on Brigitte Bardot, 1983*

When I saw him sitting behind his desk in his opulent
office, he looked just like Blake Carrington.
Fiona Wright on Sir Ralph Halpern, with whom she had an affair

FASHION

I dress for women and undress for men.
Angie Dickinson, American actress

You'd be surprised how much it costs to look this
cheap.
Dolly Parton

I tend to wear outfits that match the walls.
Debra Winger, American actress

My weakness is wearing too much leopard print.
Jackie Collins, British novelist

It is difficult to see why lace should be so expensive. It is
mostly holes.
Mary Wilson Little

Brevity is the soul of lingerie.
Dorothy Parker

Statistics are like a bikini. What they reveal is suggestive
but what they conceal is vital.
Aaron Levenstein

I know I was considered by colleagues to be somewhat
of a card. Even with the narcissistic, claustrophobic,
perfumed field of haute couture right through to the
tatty commercialism of Carnaby Street and beyond, I
was not considered the norm. My eye and judgment
were influenced too easily by the pulling power of
clothing. I couldn't endorse the sexually unappealing.
Nor push the visually drab, designed to dampen in a
puritan fashion the joyous animal urges.
Molly Parkin, British writer and journalist

Girls who wear zippers shouldn't live alone.
John W. Van Druten

Where's a man who could ease a heart like a satin
gown?
Dorothy Parker

In olden days a glimpse of stocking was looked on as
something shocking but now, God knows, Anything
goes.
Cole Porter

FAUX PAS

I'll give you a clue. His name sounds like something
hard that tastes good when you suck it.
Game-show host **Chris Tarrant**, *trying to help a contestant name
a famous motor-racing commentator (the answer was Murray
Walker). The contestant's reply? 'Ah, it must be Dickie Davies'*

Forty seconds on the cock.
Henry Kelly *to a female contestant on the TV show* Going for
Gold

Does your friend always give you one before you
appear on TV?
Bob Holness, *host of TV quiz show* Blockbusters, *asking about a
contestant's mascot which had been given to her by a friend*

FEMINISM

If you catch a man throw him back.
Australian Women's liberation slogan, 1970

Adam was a rough draft.
Anon

A liberated woman is one who has sex before marriage
and a job after.
Gloria Steinem, *American feminist writer and critic*

No man is as anti-feminist as a really feminine woman.
Frank O'Connor

Remember, Ginger Rogers did everything Fred Astaire
did, but backwards and in high heels.
Faith Whittlesey

I myself have never been able to find out precisely what
feminism is: I only know that people call me a feminist
whenever I express sentiments that differentiate me
from a doormat.
Rebecca West

The only question left to be settled now is: are women persons?
Susan B. Anthony

But if God wanted us to think with our wombs, why did he give us a brain?
Clare Boothe Luce (1903-87), *American journalist, playwright and politician*

If men could get pregnant, abortion would be a sacrament.
Florynce Kennedy

Take your secretary to lunch. He'll appreciate it.
Anon

Sometimes the best man for the job isn't.
Anon

In the world we live in feminism is a trivial cause.
Doris Lessing, *British novelist*

Women's liberation is just a lot of foolishness. It's men who are discriminated against. They can't bear children. And no one's likely to do anything about that.
Golda Meir (1898-1987), *Israeli politician and former prime minister*

Whatever women do they must do twice as well as men to be thought half as good. Luckily, this is not difficult.
Charlotte Whitton on becoming Mayor of Ottawa

I would rather lie on the sofa than sweep beneath it.
Shirley Conran

Beware of the man who praises women's liberation; he is about to quit his job.
Erica Jong

Scratch most feminists and underneath there is a woman who longs to be a sex object. The difference is that is not *all* she longs to be.
Betty Rollin

The major concrete achievement of the Women's Movement of the 1970s was the Dutch Treat.
Nora Ephron

I'm furious with women's liberationists. They keep
getting up on soapboxes and proclaiming that women
are brighter than men. That's true, but it should be kept
very quiet or it ruins the whole racket.
Anita Loos

Women are the only exploited group in history to have
been idealized into powerlessness.
Erica Jong

No one should have to dance backward all of their
lives.
Jill Ruckelshaus, Amrican government official and lecturer

Despite a lifetime of service to the cause of sexual
liberation, I have never caught venereal disease, which
makes me feel rather like an Arctic explorer who has
never had frostbite.
Germaine Greer

If you want to know, I'm really tired of feminists, sick
of them. They've really dug themselves into their own
grave. Any man would be a fool who didn't agree with
equal rights and pay, but some women now, juggling
with career, lover, children, wifehood, have spread
themselves too thin and are very unhappy.
Michael Douglas, American actor and film producer

Wife: Cooking! Cleaning! Why should women do it?
Husband: You're right – let's get an au pair girl.
Mel Calman, Couples *cartoon, 1972*

We had taken the first step along the tortuous road that
led to the sex war, sado-masochism, and ultimately to
the whole contemporary snarl-up, to prostitution,
prudery, Casanova, John Knox, Marie Stopes, white
slavery, Women's Liberation, *Playboy* magazine, *crimes
passionels*, censorship, strip clubs, alimony,
pornography, and a dozen different brands of mania.
This was the Fall. It had nothing to do with apples.
Elain Morgan, *Welsh writer*, The Descent of Women, *1972*

The Women's Movement hasn't changed my sex life at
all. It wouldn't dare.
Zsa Zsa Gabor

Never go to bed mad. Stay up and fight.
Phyllis Diller

To me, the important task of modern feminism is to
accept and proclaim sex: to bury for ever the lie that the
body is a hindrance to the mind, and sex is a necessary
evil to be endured for the perpetuation of our race.
Dora Russell, *British writer*

When a woman behaves like a man, why can't she
behave like a nice man?
Dame Edith Evans, *British actress*

I'm the most liberated woman in the world. Any
woman can be liberated if she wants to be. First, she has
to convince her husband.
Martha Mitchell

FLIRT

Flirt: a woman who thinks it's every man for herself.
Anon

My heart is a bargain today. Will you take it?
W. C. Fields

She'll be on more laps than a napkin.
Walter Winchell

No matter how happily a woman may be married, it
always pleases her to discover that there is a nice man
who wishes that she were not.
H. L. Mencken

Ah, beautiful passionate body that has never ached with
a heart!
A. C. Swinburne *(1837-1909), English poet*

What attracts us in a woman rarely binds us to her.
J. Churton Collins

Men do make passes at girls who wear glasses – but it
all depends on their frames.
Optician, 1964

In order to avoid being called a flirt, she always yielded
easily.
Charles Talleyrand *(1754-1838), French politician*

FOLLY

When lovely woman stoops to folly, and finds too late
that men betray, what charm can soothe her
melancholy, what art can wash her guilt away?
Oliver Goldsmith (1728-74), Irish-born writer, The Vicar of
Wakefield, *1761-62*

Man should be trained for war and women for
recreation of the warrior: all else is folly.
Friedrich Nietzsche (1844-1900), German philosopher, Thus
Spake Zarathustra, *1883-85*

FOOD

A gourmet who thinks of calories is like a tart who
looks at her watch.
*James, American food writer, quoted beneath his picture in
Charlie O's Bar, New York*

Too many cooks spoil the brothel.
Polly Adler, American madame, A House is not a Home, *1953*

Great food is like great sex – the more you have the
more you want.
Gail Greene, American food critic, 1979

Before I was born my mother was in great agony of
spirit and in a tragic situation. She could take no food
except iced oysters and champagne. If people ask me
when I began to dance, I reply, in my mother's womb,
probably as a result of the oysters and champagne – the
food of Aphrodite.
Isadora Duncan (1878-1927), American dancer and teacher

Cooking is like love. It should be entered into with
abandon or not at all.
Harriet Van Horne, American columnist

Large naked raw carrots are acceptable as food only to
those who live in hutches eagerly awaiting Easter.
Fran Lebowitz, American writer

There is no spectacle on earth more appealing than that
of a beautiful woman in the act of cooking dinner for
someone she loves.
Thomas Wolfe (1900-38), American author

. . . Unnecessary dieting is because everything from
television to fashion ads has made it seem wicked to
cast a shadow. This wild, emaciated look appeals to
some women, though not to many men, who are
seldom seen pinning up a *Vogue* illustration in a
machine shop.
Peg Bracken, American humorist

The right diet directs sexual energy into the parts that
matter
Barbara Cartland

FOREPLAY

How a man must hug, and dandle, and kittle, and play
a hundred little tricks with his bedfellow when he is
disposed to make that use of her that nature designed
for her.
Erasmus (1466-1536), Dutch humanist, scholar and writer, The
Praise of Folly, 1511

Girls like to be played with and rumpled a little too,
sometimes.
Oliver Goldsmith

The 1950s were ten years of foreplay.
Germaine Greer

Not for her potatoes
and pudding made of rice
she takes carbohydrates
like God takes advice.
A surfeit of ambition
is her particular vice
Valerie fondles lovers
Like a mousetrap fondles mice.
Roger McGough, Discretion, 1967

Half the time, if you really want to know the truth,
when I'm horsing around and with a girl, I have a
helluva lot of trouble just finding what I'm looking for,
for God's sake, if you know what I mean. Take this girl
that I just mentioned having sexual intercourse with,
that I told you about. It took me about an hour just to
get her Goddam brassiere off, she was about ready to
spit in my eye.
Holden Caulfield *in* The Catcher in the Rye, *by* J. D. Salinger,
1951

There is no petting . . . Modern couples just strip their clothes and go at it . . . blame must . . . be placed on ex-President Nixon's decision to let the US dollar float in relation to other western currencies. More than a decade of monetary instability has conditioned people to utilise their assets immediately. If the sex urge is not spent forthwith, it might degenerate into something less valuable – affection, for instance.
P. J. O'Rourke, Modern Manners

She tried to pull me once. Her thing was to hang from my minstrel gallery and swing like some great bat, while murmuring sexy things at me. This was supposed to turn me on but the effect it actually had was to make me run upstairs and lock the darkroom door . . . These were very big ladies. It made me feel inadequate.
*Hippy photographer **Keith Morris** describing his relationship with Germaine Greer in the 1960s. (Quoted in the* Encyclopedia of Erotic Failure*)*

Nell Gwynn, lover and patron of Charles II, discovering a rival had been invited to the King's bed, entertained the woman at a pre-coital dinner where she doctored her meal with 'physical ingredients' . . . The effect thereof had such an operation upon the harlot, when the King was caressing her in bed with amorous sports of Venus, that a violent and sudden looseness obliging her ladyship to discharge her artillery, she made the King, as well as herself in a most lamentable pickle.
*Reported by **Alexander Smith** in* The School of Venus

Kissing, fondling and foreplay are regarded as the height of bad behaviour among the tribe and its culture contains not one romantic song or story. There is no Manuan word for 'love'.
***Margaret Mead**, anthropologist, describing the Manus tribe of the Admiralty Islands*

FRIENDSHIP

Friendship is a disinterested commerce between equals; love, an abject intercourse between tyrants and slaves.
Oliver Goldsmith

He's the kind of man who picks his friends – to pieces.
Mae West

Platonic friendship – the interval between the
introduction and the first kiss.
Sophie Irene Loeb

Most friendship is feigning, most loving mere folly.
William Shakespeare *(1564-1616)*, As You Like It, *1600*

Her friendships were flames of extravagant passion
ending in aversion.
Sarah Churchill *(1914-82), British actress and author, on Queen
Anne*

Friendship between men and women can be a tricky
business because a pretty face all too easily attracts a
weak soul, and visual temptation kindles carnal lust,
often to produce a defiled mind and body. Familiarity
between men and women is apt to turn to virtue's
disadvantage.
Richard Rolle *(c.1300-49), English writer,* The Fire of Love,
fourteenth century

I have always detested the belief that sex is the chief
bond between man and woman. Friendship is far more
human.
Agnes Smedley *(c.1894-1950), American author and lecturer,*
Battle Hymn of China, *1943*

FUN

Most of the time I don't have much fun. The rest of the
time I don't have any fun at all.
Woody Allen

The game women play is men.
Adam Smith

People must not do things for fun. We are not here for
fun. There is no reference to fun in any Act of
Parliament.
A. P. Herbert *(1890-1971), British author and politician*

Eric: It was a gay nineties party. It was terrible.
Ernie: Why was that?
Eric: All the men were gay and all the women were
ninety.
The Eric Morecambe and Ernie Wise Joke Book

The proliferation of massage establishments in London in the last few years appears to indicate a dramatic increase in muscular disorders amongst the male population.
Anonymous Environmental Health officer quoted in the New Statesman *magazine, 1980*

Setting a good example for your children takes all the fun out of middle age.
William Feather, *American businessman*, The Business of Life, 1949

GOSSIP

If you haven't got anything nice to say about anybody, come sit next to me.
Alice Roosevelt Longworth (1884-1980)

She'll wear the pants in that marriage.
Harvey Smith, British show jumper, on Princess Anne

Men have always detested women's gossip because they suspect the truth about their measurements being taken and compared.
Erica Jong, American poet and writer, Fear of Flying, 1973

HABIT

Teenagers and old people may know how to dance, but real people who go to real parties haven't the slightest. The only dances they even half-remember how to do are the ones they learned twenty years ago. This is what the old Supremes tape is for: still and overweight versions of the Jerk, the Mashed Potato, the Pony, the Swim, and the Watusi. And after six drinks everyone will revert to the Twist.
P. J. O'Rourke, Modern Manners, 1983

Like so many substantial Americans, he had married young and kept on marrying, stringing from blonde to blonde like the chamois of the Alps leaping from crag to crag.
P. G. Wodehouse (1881-1975), British humorist and novelist

Just as old habits die hard, old hards die habits.
Kenneth Tynan on pornography, Esquire *magazine, 1968*

Oh my God, what are you doing down there? Get off! Get off!
Film director **Michael Curtiz**, *discovered by his cast and crew in an unbuttoned moment. The Hungarian-born director of such films as* Casablanca *and* The Adventures of Robin Hood *was in the habit of relaxing during his lunch-break on the set with a glass of wine, a sandwich and a spot of oral sex supplied by one of the make-up girls*

HAPPINESS

The happiness of man is: I will. The happiness of women is: he wills.
Friedrich Nietzsche

When I was a small child . . . I thought that success spelled happiness. I was wrong. Happiness is like a butterfly which appears and delights us for one brief moment, but soon flits away.
Anna Pavlova (1881-1931), Russian ballet dancer

It is only possible to live happily ever after on a day-to-day basis.
Margaret Bonnano

HATE

I never hated a man enough to give him his diamonds back.
Zsa Zsa Gabor

Malice is like a game of poker or tennis; you don't play it with anyone who is manifestly inferior to you.
Hilde Spiel

HOLLYWOOD

You can seduce a man's wife there, attack his daughter and wipe your hands on his canary, but if you don't like his movie, you're dead.
Joseph von Sternberg, American director

Hollywood's a place where they'll pay you a thousand dollars for a kiss, and fifty cents for your soul.
Marilyn Monroe

If we have to kiss Hollywood goodbye, it may be with one of those tender, old-fashioned, seven-second kisses as exchanged between two people of the opposite sex with all their clothes on.
Anita Loos (1893-1981), American screenwriter

HOMOSEXUALITY

It was out of the closet and into the streets for the nation's homosexuals in the 1970s. This didn't do much for the streets but, on the other hand, your average closet was improved immeasurably.
Richard Meyerowitz and John Weidman, National Lampoon, 1980

If homosexuality were the normal way, God would have made Adam and Bruce.
Anita Bryant, American anti-Gay Rights campaigner

I became one of the stately homos of England.
Quentin Crisp, British writer, The Naked Civil Servant, 1968

Homosexuality is a sickness, just as are baby-rape or wanting to become the head of General Motors.
Eldridge Cleaver, Soul on Ice, 1968

This sort of thing may be tolerated by the French – but we are British, thank God.
Viscount Montgomery (1887-1976), British soldier

There is probably no sensitive heterosexual alive who is not preoccupied with his latent homosexuality.
Norman Mailer, American writer

Postumus, are you really taking a wife? . . . Isn't it better to sleep with a pretty boy? Boys don't quarrel all night, or nag you for little presents while they're on the job, or complain that you don't come up to their expectations, or demand more gasping passion.
Juvenal, Roman satirist, Satires VI, first century AD

Texas Woman: Are you a homosexual? We don't have homosexuals in Texas – live ones, anyway.
Susan Harris, Soap, ABC TV, 1978

I'd rather be black than gay because when you're black you don't have to tell your mother.
Charles Pierce, American female impersonator

Gay whales against the bomb.
London badge slogan, 1982

My favourite city is San Francisco because it's gay. They teach the kids in school: AC . . . DC . . . EFG . . .
Joan Rivers

As a mother, I know that homosexuals cannot biologically produce children, therefore they must recruit our children.
Anita Bryant

Homosexuals have the time for everybody . . . every detail of lives of real people, however mundane it may be, seems romantic to them.
Quentin Crisp, British writer, The Naked Civil Servant, 1968

We didn't go for the gay concept when we put the show together. We went for a totally male, masculine celebration – that men can get up there and feel their tits and do bumps and grinds and still remain men. Narcissism is a good thing. Everybody does it, I don't care what they say. Everyone gets off on mirror-tripping.
David 'Scar' Hodo, a member of the American disco group, The Village People

I was too polite to ask.
*Gore Vidal, American writer, on being asked by David Frost
whether his first sexual experience had been heterosexual or
homosexual*

I cover the waterfront.
*Tennessee Williams, American playwright, on being asked by
David Frost if he was homosexual*

This is a celebration of individual freedom, not of
homosexuality. No government has the right to tell its
citizens when or whom to love. The only queer people
are those who don't love anybody.
*Rita Mae Brown, American feminist writer, at the Gay
Olympics, 1982*

People who have a low self esteem . . . have a tendency
to cling to their own sex because it is less frightening.
*Clara Thompson (1893-1958), American physician, psychiatrist
and educator*

HUMOUR

Do you come here often? Only in the mating season.
Spike Milligan in The Goon Show

My father told me all about the birds and the bees, the
liar – I went steady with a woodpecker till I was twenty-
one.
Bob Hope

Those hot pants of hers were so damned tight, I could
hardly breathe.
Benny Hill, British comedian

He looks like he's got a cheese danish stuffed in his
pants!
Tom Wolfe, American writer, Bonfire of the Vanities

A one-time US Ambassador in Europe, astonishing in
view of his age, is said to have approached all problems
with a closed mind and an open fly.
John Kenneth Galbraith, British writer and economist

Please, Sir John, does that apply to those of us who only
have small parts?
*A member of the cast to Sir John Gielgud, who had told them that
all the men must wear jock-straps under their leotards*

No, the 'T' is silent – as in Harlow.
Margot Asquith to Jean Harlow – apparently, the actress had not encountered the name 'Margot' before and asked if the 'T' was pronounced or not

Comedy, like sodomy, is an unnatural act.
Marty Feldman, quoted in The Times, *1969*

I'm never vulgar. I kid sex. I take it out in the open and laugh at it.
Mae West

Wit in women is apt to have bad consequences; like a sword without a scabbard, it wounds the wearer and provokes assailants. I am sorry to say the generality of women who have excelled in wit have failed in chastity.
Elizabeth Montagu (1720-1800), British essayist, Reconstructing Aphra

I thought *coq au vin* was love in a lorry.
Victoria Wood, comedian and playwright, Talent, *1979*

I am not interested in an inanimate statue of a little bald man. I like something with long blonde curls.
Woody Allen, American actor and film director, refusing to attend the Oscars ceremony, 1978

She sleeps alone at last.
Robert Benchley (1889-1945), American humorist, suggesting an epitaph for a certain actress

Women find men who have a sense of humour *extremely* sexy. You don't have to look like Robert Redford. All you have to do is tickle her funny bone, and she'll follow you anywhere. If you can make her laugh, you've got it made! *Man*: One to call her dad and the other to open her Diet Pepsi! *Woman*: Oh, stop! You're killing me! Take off your clothes, quick!
Mimi Pond, Mimi Pond's Secrets of the Powder Room

HUSBANDS

I've been asked to say a couple of words about my husband Fang. How about 'short' and 'cheap'.
Phyllis Diller

He tells you when you've got too much lipstick, and
helps you with your girdle when your hips stick.
Ogden Nash (1902-71), American poet, The Perfect Husband,
1949

A woman usually respects her father, but her view of
her husband is mingled with contempt, for she is of
course privy to the transparent devices by which she
snared him.
H. L. Mencken

No one asks how his marriage survives if he's away.
*Angela Rippon, in reply to interviewer who asked if living apart
puts a strain on a relationship*

A small band of men armed only with wallets, besieged
by a horde of wives and children.
National Lampoon, *1979*

The way to hold a husband is to keep him a little
jealous; the way to lose him is to keep him a little more
jealous.
H. L. Mencken

American husbands are the best in the world; no other
husbands are so generous to their wives, or can be so
easily divorced.
Elinor Glyn

Husbands think we should know where everything is –
like the uterus is the tracking device. He asks me,
'Roseanne, do we have any che-tos left?' Like he can't
go over to that sofa cushion and lift it himself.
Roseanne Barr, American actress and comedienne

One exists with one's husband – one lives with one's
lover.
Honoré de Balzac (1799-1850), French novelist and critic

I think every woman is entitled to a middle husband she
can forget.
Adela Rogers St John

A husband is what is left of the lover after the nerve is
extracted.
Helen Rowland

There is so little difference between husbands you might
as well keep the first.
Adela Rogers St John

Before I met him, I wasn't used to the fact that buying
the wrong length shoelaces would be the reason to
contemplate suicide.
*Sarah Woods talking about the moodiness of her estranged
husband, actor James Woods*

I have three pets at home which answer to the same
purpose as a husband: I have a dog which growls every
morning, a parrot which swears all afternoon and a cat
that comes home late at night.
Marie Corelli

An archaeologist is the best husband any woman can
have; the older she gets, the more interested he is in her.
Agatha Christie

Husbands are like fire. They go out if unattended.
Zsa Zsa Gabor

If you cannot have your dear husband for a comfort
and a delight, for a breadwinner and a cross-patch, for
a sofa chair or hot water bottle, one can use him as a
cross to be borne.
Stevie Smith (1902-71), British poet

The divine right of husbands, like the divine right of
kings, may, it is hoped in this enlightened age, be
contested without danger.
Mary Wolstonecraft, A Vindication of the Rights of Women

I began as a passion and ended as a habit, like all
husbands.
George Bernard Shaw

I know many married men, I even know a few happily
married men, but I don't know one who wouldn't fall
down the first open coal hole running after the first
pretty girl who gave him a wink.
George Jean Nathan (1882-1958), American critic

Being a husband is a whole-time job. That is why so
many husbands fail. They cannot give their entire
attention to it.
Arnold Bennett (1867-1931), British novelist

The majority of husbands remind me of an orang-utan
trying to play the violin.
Honoré de Balzac (1799-1850)

A good husband makes a good wife.
Robert Burton

Husbands never become good. They merely become proficient.
H. L. Mencken

Nothing flatters a man as much as the happiness of his wife; he is always proud of himself as the source of it.
Dr Samuel Johnson

Every man who is high up likes to think he has done it all himself, and the wife smiles and lets it go at that.
J. M. Barrie

The concern that some women show at the absence of their husbands does not arise from their not seeing them and being with them, but from the apprehension that their husbands are enjoying pleasures in which they do not participate, and which, from their being at a distance, they have not the power of interrupting.
Michel de Montaigne (1533-92), French writer

The most popular labour-saving device today is still a husband with money.
Joey Adams, American comedian, Cindy and I

Celibacy is the better stake, since the best husband is not worth a fig.
Elizabeth-Charlotte, Duchess of Orleans, sister-in-law of King Louis XIV of France

When two people marry they become in the eyes of the law one person, and that one person is the husband.
Shana Alexander, American writer, State-by-State Guide to Women's Legal Rights, 1975

I do, and I also wash and iron them.
Dennis Thatcher replying to the question 'Who wears the pants in your house?', the Los Angeles Times, 1981

I have no wish for a second husband. I had enough of the first. I like to have my own way, to lie down mistress and get up master.
Susanna Moodie (1803-85), Canadian writer and poet, Epistle to a Lady

The husband who decides to surprise his wife is often very much surprised himself.
Voltaire (1694-1778), French writer

He is always dealing with beautiful women but it must be like being in a chocolate shop – after a while, you don't notice the goodies any more.
Barbara Taylor Bradford, English novelist, on her husband

I M A G I N A T I O N

Were it not for imagination, Sir, a man would be as happy in the arms of a chambermaid as of a duchess.
Dr Samuel Johnson, Life of Johnson, *vol.III, 1778*

A lady's imagination is very rapid; it jumps from admiration to love, from love to matrimony in a moment.
Jane Austen (1775-1817), English novelist

I M P O T E N C E

Thou treacherous, base deserter of my flame, false to my passion, fatal to my fame, through what mistaken magic dost thou prove so true to lewdness, so untrue to love?
John Wilmot, Earl of Rochester

I M P R E S S I O N S

She has as much originality as a Xerox machine.
Laurence J. Peter

Hubert Humphrey talks so fast that listening to him is like trying to read *Playboy* magazine with your wife turning the pages.
Barry Goldwater, American politician

I N F A T U A T I O N

Many a man in love with a dimple makes the mistake of marrying the wrong girl.
Stephen Leacock, English-born Canadian economist and humorist, Literary Lapses, 1910

Infatuation is when you think that he's as sexy as
Robert Redford, as smart as Henry Kissinger, as noble
as Ralph Nader, as funny as Woody Allen and as
athletic as Jimmy Connors. Love is when you realise
that he's as sexy as Woody Allen, as smart as Jimmy
Connors, as funny as Ralph Nader, as athletic as Henry
Kissinger and nothing like Robert Redford – but you'll
take him anyway.
Judith Viorist, Redbook, 1975

INFIDELITY

I have always held that it was a very good thing for a
young girl to fall hopelessly in love with a married man
so that, later on and in the opposite predicament, she
could remember what an unassailable citadel a marriage
can be.
Katherine Whithorn

A man does not look behind the door unless he has
stood there himself.
Henri du Bois

When a man steals your wife, there is no better revenge
than to let him keep her.
Sacha Guitry

Husbands are chiefly good lovers when they are
betraying their wives.
Marilyn Monroe

It is better to be unfaithful than to be faithful without
wanting to be.
Brigitte Bardot

If your home burns down, rescue the dogs. At least
they'll be faithful to you.
Lee Marvin, American actor

Never tell. Not if you love your wife . . . In fact, if your
old lady walks in on you deny it. Yeah. Just flat out
she'll believe it: I'm tellin' ya. This chick came
downstairs with a sign around her neck: 'Lay On Top
Of Me Or I'll Die.' I didn't know what I was gonna
do . . .
Lenny Bruce

One man's folly is another man's wife.
Helen Rowland

I didn't want to upset my marriage. The best way I
could satisfy a man's urge was to pick on somebody
who would not be a threat to my wife.
*Sir Ralph Halpern on his much-publicised affair with model
Fiona Wright.*

I could never have sex with any man who has so little
regard for my husband.
Title of film by Dan Greenburg

I said to the wife, guess what I heard in the pub? They
reckon the milkman has made love to every woman in
this road except one. And she said, I'll bet it's that
stuck-up Phyllis at number twenty-three.
Max Kauffmann

There is one thing I would break up over, and that is if
she caught me with another woman. I won't stand for
that.
Steve Martin, American actor and comedian

Your idea of fidelity is not having more than one man
in bed at the same time.
Dirk Bogarde in the film Darling *(screenplay by Frederic Raphael)*

Accursed from their birth they be
Who seek to find monogamy
Pursuing it from bed to bed –
I think they would be better dead.
Dorothy Parker

Sara could commit adultery at one end and weep for
her sins at the other, and enjoy both operations at once.
Joyce Cary (1888-1957), British novelist

Benchley and I had an office in the old *Life* magazine
that was so tiny, if it were an inch smaller it would have
been adultery.
Dorothy Parker

I have looked on a lot of women with lust. I've
committed adultery in my heart many times. God
recognises I will do this and forgives me.
Jimmy Carter, former American president

What men call Gallantry, and the Gods adultery, is much more common when the climate's sultry.
Lord Byron *(1788-1824), English poet,* Don Juan

Thou shall not commit adultery . . . unless in the mood.
W. C. Fields

Eric: She's a lovely girl . . . I'd like to marry her, but her family objects.
Ernie: Her family?
Eric: Yes, her husband and four kids.
Morecambe and Wise Joke Book

A father will have compassion on his son. A mother will never forget her child. A brother will cover the sin of his sister. But what husband ever forgave the faithlessness of his wife?
Queen Margaret of Navarre *(1492-1549), French poet and writer,* Mirror of the Sinful Soul, *1531*

Of course I've known for years our marriage has been a mockery. My body lying there night after night in the wasted moonlight. I know now how the Taj Mahal must feel.
Mrs Wicksteed in Habeas Corpus *by Alan Bennett, 1973*

INSULTS

If there's a worse insult, I don't know it. I have just been told by my friend Gladys that she'd trust her husband to spend an evening alone with me.
Marjorie Proops, British journalist and broadcaster

No, the 'T' is silent – as in Harlow.
Margot Asquith to Jean Harlow – apparently, the actress had not encountered the name 'Margot' before and asked if the 'T' was pronounced or not

With a head like yours I am surprised you don't get it circumcised.
Pamela Armstrong, TV newscaster, in reply to a heckler during a speech she was making at Cambridge University Union

Eric: Who was that lady I seen you with last night?
Ernie: You mean, 'I saw'.
Eric: Sorry. Who was that eyesore I seen you with last night?
The Morecambe and Wise Joke Book, *1979*

Firefly (Groucho Marx): Oh, er, I suppose you'll think me a sentimental old fluff, but, er, would you mind giving me a lock of your hair?
Mrs Teasdale: A lock of my hair? Why I had no idea . . .
Firefly: I'm letting you off easy. I was going to ask for the whole wig.
From the film Duck Soup, *1933 (screenplay by Arthur Sheekman and Nat Perrin)*

INTIMACY

If ever a man and his wife, or a man and his mistress, who pass nights as well as days together, absolutely lay aside all good breeding, their intimacy will soon degenerate into a coarse familiarity.
Lord Chesterfield (1694-1773)

To really know someone is to have loved and hated him
in turn.
Marcel Jouhandeau (1888-1979), French writer

INNUENDO

Never do with your hands what you could do better
with your mouth.
Cherry Vanilla, American groupie

Wink, wink, nudge, nudge, say no more, know what I
mean . . .
Catchphrase of British comedian Eric Idle in Monty Python's
Flying Circus, *the TV show*

IRONY

Woman is: finally screwing and your groin and
buttocks and thighs ache like hell and you're all wet and
bloody and it wasn't like a Hollywood movie at all, but
Jesus, at least your not a virgin anymore – but is that
what it's all about? And meanwhile he's asking, 'Did
you come?'
Robin Morgan, American feminist

A fox is a wolf who sends flowers.
Ruth Weston, American actress

He sleeps fastest who sleeps alone.
Richard Avedon, American photographer

A twenty-five-year-old virgin is like the man who was
set upon by thieves – everyone passes by.
Charlotte Bingham, British writer

Everyone has experienced that truth: that love, like a
running brook, is disregarded, taken for granted; but
when the brook freezes over, then people begin to
remember how it was when it ran, and they want it to
run again.
Kahil Gibran (1833-1931), Lebanese mystic and poet, Beloved
Prophet *(ed. Virginia Hilu, c.1930)*

Love is based on a view that is impossible to those who
have had any experience with them.
H. L. Mencken (1880-1956), American journalist and humorist

Literature is mostly about having sex and not much about having children; life is the other way round.
David Lodge, British author, The British Museum is Falling Down, *1965*

J E A L O U S Y

Jealousy is the fear of losing the thing you love most. It's very normal. Suspicion is the thing that's abnormal.
Jerry Hall, American actress and model

People may go on talking for ever of the jealousies of pretty women; but for real genuine hard-working envy, there is nothing like an ugly woman with a taste for admiration.
Emily Eden (1797-1869), British-born Indian novelist, The Semi-Detached Couple, *1830*

I think the only jealousy worth having is sexual jealousy. If I find something out, I go. I'm not a masochist. I don't hang around.
Jean Marsh, English actress

K I N K Y

Business lady and gentleman would like to rent ground-floor rooms or flat in North London in order to breed a litter of wire fox-terriers, very careful tenants, no children.
Advertisement placed in Our Dogs *magazine*

I gave her a sheer negligee and she let me put it on. But I don't look good in a sheer negligee.
Anon

Are you fond of nuts? Is this a proposal?
Anon

Kinky as a very old dancing pump.
Clive James

It's always been my ambition to have a baby elephant.
Elephant keeper, London Zoo

Danny Devito went a little crazy after he put his make-up on. He would become the Penguin. Once he had his beak on, we had to stop him biting anybody who came near him.
Tim Burton, *director of the film* Batman Returns

I only used to bite one person, and that was Michelle Pfeiffer. And every guy would like to do that . . .
Danny Devito, *actor, denying Burton's allegation*

Corrie: There isn't the least bit of adventure in you. You're a watcher. There are watchers in this world and there are do-ers. And the watchers sit around watching the do-ers do. Well, tonight you watched and I did.
Paul: Yeah . . . well, it was harder to watch what you did than it was for you to do what I was watching.
From Barefoot in the Park *by Neil Simon, 1964*

I get letters, sometimes scores of them a week, asking if I am available, available on my own. Available with wardrobe. Available with my husband. Available back, front, side and arse-ways up. In short – do I swing? I don't know that's the trouble, I speak a lot instead.
Molly Parkin, Good Golly Miss Molly

If you are looking for a really fascinating, out-of-the-ordinary pet, may we suggest you visit the speciality section and ask to see our Miss Mortimore?
Manchester Evening News

Y-Fronts wanted. No questions asked. Interesting career possibilities.
Henley Standard

Sex means spank and beautiful means bottom and always will.
Kenneth Tynan

See that couple over there – they're looking at you, behave.
Poet-Laureate **John Betjeman** *(1906-84), to his teddy bear, Archie (sitting on his lap at the time), and surprising strangers travelling on the London Underground*

I had to give up masochism – I was enjoying it too much.
Mel Calman, Dr Calman's Dictionary of Psychoanalysis, *1979*

KISSING

It takes a lot of experience for a girl to kiss like a beginner.
Ladies Home Journal, *1948*

Lord! I wonder what fool it was that first invented kissing.
Jonathan Swift (1667-1745), Irish satirist, author and cleric

I'd love to kiss you, but I just washed my hair.
Bette Davis in the film Cabin in the Cotton

I wasn't kissing her, I was whispering in her mouth.
Chico Marx

I kissed my first girl and smoked my first cigarette on the same day. I haven't had time for tobacco since.
Arturo Toscanini (1867-1957), Italian conductor

When women kiss it always reminds one of prize fighters shaking hands.
H. L. Mencken

In love there is always one who kisses and one who offers the cheek.
French proverb

To a woman the first kiss is just the end of the beginning, but to a man it is the beginning of the end.
Helen Rowland

The sound of a kiss is not so loud as that of a cannon, but its echo lasts a great deal longer.
Dr Oliver Wendell Holmes (1809-1894), American writer and physician

But his kiss was so sweet, and so closely he pressed, that I languished and pined till I granted the rest.
John Gay (1865-1732), English poet and playwright

The kiss originated when the first male reptile licked the first female reptile, implying in a subtle, complimentary way that she was as succulent as the small reptile he had for dinner the night before.
F. Scott Fitzgerald

Everybody winds up kissing the wrong person good night.
Andy Warhol (1928-87), American artist and film-maker

I'll scream if you touch me – explained a pert miss,
when her lover attempted an innocent kiss. But when he
gave up and made ready to go, the damsel cried louder
– I'll scream till you do.
Martial (AD 40-c.104), *Latin poet*

We did one of those quick, awkward kisses where each
of you gets a nose in the eye.
Clive James, Unreliable Memoirs

An office party is not, as is sometimes supposed, the
managing director's chance to kiss the tea-girl. It is the
tea-girl's chance to kiss the managing director (however
bizarre an ambition this may seem to anyone who has
seen the managing director face on).
Katherine Whitehorn, *British journalist*, Roundabout

A young woman who allows herself to be kissed and
caressed goes the rest of the way too.
Elizabeth-Charlotte, *Duchess of Orleans, sister-in-law of Louis
XIV of France*

A man who spent the last eight years working with
Franciscan monks, punched a woman and hit another
when they refused to kiss him on the Edinburgh-
Glasgow train.
Report in the Glasgow Evening Times

Wherever one wants to be kissed.
Coco Chanel (1883-1971), *French fashion designer, on being
asked where one should wear perfume*

LADY

I have bursts of being a lady, but it doesn't last long. I'm the modern, intelligent, independent-type women. In other words, a girl who can't get a man.
Shelley Winters, American actress

A lady is nothing very specific. One man's lady is another man's woman; sometimes, one man's lady is another man's wife. Definitions overlap but they almost never coincide.
Russell Lynes, American editor and critic

A lady is one who never shows her underwear unintentionally.
Lillian Day, American writer

LAW

There are only about twenty murders a year in London and many not at all serious – some are just husbands killing their wives.
Commander G. H. Hatherill of Scotland Yard, 1954

Legislation and case law still exist in some parts of the United States permitting the 'passion shooting by husband of a wife'; the reverse, of course, is known as homicide.
Diane B. Schulder, American lawyer and educator, in Sisterhood is Powerful (ed. Robin Morgan), 1970

He would stand the chance of violent sexual abuse and becoming a homosexual if sent to a state prison.
Judge Robert C. Abel, explaining why he had given a sentence of only 120 days to a man found guilty of raping and beating a woman, 1982

I am not saying that a girl hitching home late at night should not be protected by the law, but she was guilty of a great deal of contributory negligence.
Bertrand Richards, British judge, Ipswich, 1982

LESBIANISM

My lesbianism is an act of Christian charity. All those women out there are praying for a man, and I'm giving them my share.
Rita Mae Brown, American novelist

Our sexuality is used only when film-makers want to
spice up the plot . . . we're never shown in a realistic
light.
*Lesbian activist protesting about Hollywood's unfair representation
of gay people*

Male heckler: Are you a lesbian?
Florynce Kennedy: Are you my alternative?

Girls who put out are tramps. Girls who don't are
ladies. This is, however, a rather archaic usage of the
word. Should one of you boys happen upon a girl who
doesn't put out, do not jump to the conclusion that you
have found a lady. What you have probably found is a
lesbian.
Fran Lebowitz, American journalist

Once you know what women are like, men get kind of
boring. I'm not trying to put them down, I mean I like
them sometimes as people, but sexually they're dull.
Rita Mae Brown, American novelist

Lesbianism has always seemed to me an extremely
inventive response to the shortage of men but otherwise
not worth the trouble.
Nora Ephron, Heartburn, *1983*

The Well of Loneliness, a novel by Radclyffe Hall,
which treates of intimate relationships between women,
was withdrawn on the advice of the Home Secretary, to
whom the publishers submitted it for an opinion. But
this was not before it had been condemned by the editor
of the *Sunday Express*, who declared he 'would sooner
give a healthy boy or girl a dose of prussic acid than a
copy of it'.
Report in the Daily Telegraph, *1928*

Refusal to make herself the object is not always what
turns women to homosexuality: most lesbians, on the
contrary, seek to cultivate the treasures of their
femininity.
Simone de Beauvoir, The Second Sex, *1949*

I discarded the whole book because the leading
character wasn't on my wave-length. She was a lesbian
with doubts about her masculinity.
Peter de Vries, the New York Times, *1967*

Don't say we are here because we get sexual
gratification from seeing these women playing.
Lesbian attending the Pilkington Glass Ladies Tennis
Championships 1992, in which Martina Navratilova was playing

What's the point of being a lesbian if a woman is going
to look and act like an imitation man?
Rita Mae Brown

I never said I was a dyke even to a dyke because there
wasn't a dyke in the land who thought she should be a
dyke or even thought she was a dyke so how could we
talk about it.
Jill Johnston, *British-born American writer and feminist,* Lesbian
Nation, *1973*

LIES

By the time you say you're his
Shivering and sighing
And he vows his passion is
Infinite, undying –
Lady, make a note of this
One of you is lying.
Dorothy Parker

The tombstone is about the only thing that can stand
upright and lie on its face at the same time.
Mary Wilson Little

He led a double life. Did that make him a liar? He did
not feel a liar. He was a man of two truths.
Iris Murdoch, Irish-born British novelist, The Sacred and Profane
Love Machine

Only lies and evil come from letting people off.
Iris Murdoch, A Severed Head

L I F E

If I had my life to live again, I'd make the same mistakes
only sooner.
Tallulah Bankhead (1903-68), American actress

A lot of love-making and a little abuse; a little fame and
more abuse; a real man and great happiness; the love of
children and seventh heaven; an early death and a
crowded memorial service.
Margot Asquith (1864-1945), summing up her life

L O O K S

She wore far too much rouge last night and not quite
enough clothes. That is always a sign of despair in a
woman.
Oscar Wilde, An Ideal Husband, *1895*

She wore a short skirt and a tight sweater and her figure
described a set of parabolas that could cause cardiac
arrest in a yak.
Woody Allen, Getting Even, *1973*

It was a blonde. A blonde to make a bishop kick a hole
in a stained-glass window.
Raymond Chandler (1888-1959), American novelist Farewell,
My Lovely, *1940*

She was a vivacious girl, not pretty by any accepted
standards, if anything ugly by any accepted standards,
but she could speak Latin and foot a quadrille and
sometimes the two simultaneously if the tempo was
right.
Denis Norden, Upon My Word, *1974*

She got her looks from her father – he's a plastic
surgeon.
Groucho Marx

The less I behave like Whistler's mother the night
before, the more I look like her the morning after.
Tallulah Bankhead

Just like Winnie;
like a barracks in a pinny,
gave up food for Lent,
weight loss was fantastic,
but her skin was not elastic,
like an inefficient camper in a creased pink tent.
Victoria Wood

. . . so dreadfully dowdy that she reminded one of a
badly bound hymn-book.
Oscar Wilde

Wearing very tight striped pants, he looked like a
bifurcated marrow . . . like a pensionable cherub.
Clive James on Rod Stewart

Young and handsome . . . looks like his teeth will stay
in all night.
Victoria Wood describing an ideal man

A woman with cut hair is a filthy spectacle, and much
like a monster; and all repute it a very great absurdity
for a woman to walk abroad with shorn hair; for this is
all one as if she should take upon her the form or
person of a man, to whom short cut hair is proper.
William Prynne (1600-69), English puritan, Histrioastix, 1669

L O V E

Just another four-letter word.
Tennessee Williams

If two people love each other there can be no happy end
to it.
Ernest Hemingway (1898-1961), American writer

Love is like quicksilver in the hand. Leave the fingers
open and it stays. Clutch it, and it darts away.
Dorothy Parker

To fall in love you have to be in a state of mind for it to take, like a disease.
Nancy Mitford (1904-73), *British writer*

I could follow him around the world in my shift.
Mary, Queen of Scots on James Hepburn, Earl of Bothwell

If it is your time love will track you down like a Cruise missile. If you say 'No! I don't want it right now', that's when you'll get it for sure. Love will make a way out of no way. Love is an exploding cigar which we willingly smoke.
Lynda Barry

Love is so much better when you are not married.
Maria Callas (1923-77), *opera singer*

Everything we do in life is based on fear, especially love.
Mel Brooks, *American film director*

Fantasy love is much better than reality love. Never doing it is exciting. The most exciting attractions are between two opposites that never meet.
Andy Warhol

People in love, it is well known, suffer extreme conceptual delusions; the most common of these being that other people find your condition as thrilling and eye-watering as you do yourselves.
Julian Barnes, *British novelist*

I can see from your utter misery, from your eagerness to misunderstand each other, and from your thoroughly bad temper, that this is the real thing.
Peter Ustinov, Ramanoff & Juliet, *1957*

Love is much nicer to be in than an automobile accident, a tight girdle, a higher tax bracket or a holding pattern over Philadelphia.
Judith Viorist, Redbook, *1975*

I can understand companionship. I can understand bought sex in the afternoon. I cannot understand the love affair.
Gore Vidal, *American writer and critic*

I have never loved anyone for love's sake, except perhaps Josephine – a little.
Napoleon Bonaparte

I love Mickey Mouse more than any woman I've ever known.
Walt Disney

Love is a universal migraine
A bright stain on the vision
Blotting out reason
Robert Graves (1895-1985), English poet and writer

Love is the irresistible desire to be irresistibly desired.
Robert Frost (1874-1963), American poet

Desperate madness.
John Ford, film director

Romantic love is mental illness. But it's a pleasurable one. It's a drug. It distorts reality, and that's the point of it. It would be impossible to fall in love with someone that you really saw.
Fran Lebowitz

Love has no great influences upon the sum of life.
Dr Samuel Johnson

If the rustle of a woman's petticoat has ever stirred my blood, of what matter is that to any reader?
Anthony Trollope (1815-82), English novelist, on being asked why no reference to love appeared in his two-volume autobiography

Love: woman's eternal spring and man's eternal fall.
Helen Rowland

If love be good, from whence cometh my woe?
Chaucer (c.1340-1400), English poet

Love is what you feel for a dog or a pussycat. It doesn't apply to humans.
Johnny Rotten (aka John Lydon)

You need someone to love you, while you're looking for someone to love.
Shelagh Delaney, English writer

'Yes,' I answered you last night;
'No,' this morning, Sir I say.
Colours seen by candlelight
will not look the same by day.
Elizabeth Barrett Browning (1806-61), English poet

A grave mental disease.
Plato

It's the nature of women not to love when we love
them, and to love when we love them not.
Migeul de Cervantes *(1547-1616), Spanish playwright, poet and
novelist*

Had we never lov'd sae kindly,
Had we never lov'd sae blindly,
Never met – or never parted,
We had ne'er been broken hearted.
Robert Burns, Ae Fond Kiss

Love is an ocean of emotions entirely surrounded by
expenses.
Lord Dewar

Night of love descend!
Make me forget that I am alive.
Richard Wagner *(1813-83), German opera composer,* Tristan und
Isolde, *1865*

The heart can do anything.
Molière *(1622-73), French playwright and actor*

Love is often a consequence of marriage.
Molière, Sganarelle

The whole pleasure of love lies in the variety.
Molière, Don Juan

The heaviest object in the world is the body of the
woman you have ceased to love.
Marquis de Luc de Clapiers Vauenargues *(1715-47)*

A man can be happy with any woman as long as he
does not love her.
Oscar Wilde

I sold my memoirs of my love life to Parker Brothers
and they are going to make a game out of it.
Woody Allen

In literature as in love we are astonished at what is
chosen by others.
André Maurois *(1885-1967), French novelist and writer*

Never forget that the most powerful force on earth is
love.
Nelson Rockefeller *to Henry Kissinger (1908-79)*

Love doesn't make the world go round. Love is what makes the ride worthwhile.
Franklin P. Jones

Platonic love is love from the neck up.
Thyra Smater Winsolow

Let there be spaces in your togetherness.
Kahil Gibran

Religion has done love a great service by making it a sin.
Anatole France

Take away love and our earth is a tomb.
Robert Browning (1812-89), British poet

I had a lover's quarrel with the world.
Robert Frost

The good life is one inspired by love and guided by knowledge.
Bertrand Russell (1872-1970), English philosopher

Faults are thick where love is thin.
James Howell

The head is always the dupe of the heart.
François, duc de La Rochefoucauld (1613-80), French writer

If love makes the world go round, why are we going to outer space?
Margaret Gilman

Love your enemy – it will drive him nuts.
Eleanor Doan

How absurd and delicious it is to be in love with someone younger than yourself. Everyone should try it.
Barbara Pym

A narcissism shared by two.
Rita Mae Brown

Something you have to make . . . It's all work, work.
Joyce Cary

The drug which makes sexuality palatable in popular mythology.
Germaine Greer

Love is the wisdom of the fool and the folly of the wise.
Dr Samuel Johnson (1709-84), Johnsonian Miscellanies, *1784*

Such ever was love's way; to rise, it stoops.
Robert Browning, A Death in the Desert, *1864*

Love means never having to say you're sorry.
Erich Segal, American writer, Love Story, *1970*

Don't threaten me with love, baby.
Billie Holiday (1915-59), American jazz and blues singer

Love will never be ideal until man recovers from the
illusion that he can be just a little bit faithful or a little
bit married.
Helen Rowland

Some women and men seem to need each other.
Gloria Steinem, American writer and critic

Falling out of love is very enlightening; for a short while
you see the world with new eyes.
Iris Murdoch

If you can stay in love for more than two years, you're
on something.
Fran Lebowitz

Security is when I'm very much in love with somebody
extraordinary who loves me back.
Shelley Winters

A woman that loves to be at the window is a bunch of
grapes on the highway.
English proverb

I have had two great loves in my life. Mike Todd was
the first.
Elizabeth Taylor

A woman despises a man for loving her, unless she
returns his love.
*Elizabeth Drew Stoddard (1823-1902), American novelist and
poet*

We don't believe in rheumatism and true love until after
the first attack.
Marie Ebner Von Eschenbach (1830-1916), Austrian writer,
Aphorism

Love is moral without legal marriage, but marriage is
immoral without love.
Ellen Key, The Morality of Women

It seems to me that he has never loved, that he has only
imagined that he has loved, that there has been no real
love on his part. I even think that he is incapable of
love; he is too much occupied with other thoughts and
ideas to become strongly attached to anyone earthly.
*Anna Dostoevsky (1846-1918), Russian diarist and writer, on her
husband, Fyodor Dostoevsky, the Russian novelist*

True love is like ghosts, which everyone talks about and
few have seen.
François, duc de La Rochefoucauld

People who are not in love fail to understand how an
intelligent man can suffer because of a very ordinary
woman. This is like being surprised that anyone should
be stricken with cholera because of a creature so
insignificant as the common bacillus.
Marcel Proust (1871-1922), French writer and critic

Love is a disease which fills you with a desire to be
desired.
Henri de Toulouse-Lautrec (1864-1901), French painter

The woman one loves always smells good.
Remy de Gourmont

Nuptial love maketh mankind; friendly love perfecteth
it; but wanton love corrupteth and embaseth it.
Francis Bacon (1561-1626), English philosopher, Essays Of Love,
1597

Love is the self-delusion we manufacture to justify the
trouble we take to have sex.
Dan Greenburg

Love is so different with men!
Robert Browning, In a Year, IX

Rick: I mean, what am I supposed to call you? My
girlfriend? My companion? My room-mate? Nothing
sounds quite right.
Joanie: How about your reason for living?
Rick: No, no, I need something I can use around the
office.
Garry Trudeau, creator of the 'Doonesbury Cartoons'

By the end of those six weeks, you are either in love or
you can't stand the sight of each other. But for us, it
worked out. I have such great expectations of our
future together. I have never been so happy.
*David Bowie, pop singer, on a cruise he took with his new wife
Iman (quoted in* Hello! *magazine, 1992)*

See how the poet fired with love divine,
swives in the barley, full of barley wine,
whilst in the lane, impassioned by five star,
some lawyer's at it in his Jaguar.
Robert Garioch (1909-81), poet, Love à la Mode

You've got to love something enough to kill it.
Martin Scorsese, American film director

Love is what you've been through with somebody.
James Thurber, American humorist, quoted in Life *magazine,
1960*

Love, though a very acute disorder in Andalusia, puts
on a very chronic shape in these high northern latitudes;
for first the lover must prove metaphysically that he
ought to; and then in the fifth or sixth year of courtship,
or rather argument, if the summer is tolerable warm,
and oat meal plenty, the fair one yields.
Sydney Smith in a letter to Lady Holland

Love is two minutes 52 seconds of squishing noises. It
shows your mind isn't clicking right.
Johnny Rotten

Love, love, love – all the wretched cant of it, masking
egotism, lust, masochism, fantasy under a mythology of
sentimental postures, a welter of self-induced miseries
and joys, blinding and masking the essential
personalities in the frozen gestures of courtship, in the
kissing and the dating and the desire, the compliments
and the quarrels which vivify its barrenness.
Germaine Greer, The Female Eunuch, 1970

Once a woman has given you her heart, you can never
get rid of the rest of her.
*John Vanbrugh (1664-1726), English architect and dramatist, The
Relapse, 1696*

Because women can do nothing except love, they've
given it a ridiculous importance.
W. Somerset Maugham *(1874-1965), British novelist,* The Moon
and Sixpence, *1919*

Between women love is contemplative . . . there is no
struggle no victory, no defeat; in exact reciprocity, each
is at once subject and object, sovereign and slave;
duality becomes mutuality.
Simone de Beauvoir *(1908-86), French writer,* The Second Sex,
1949

Love is a pretty kind of sporting fray,
a thing will soon away;
it is also a tooth-ache or like pain;
a game where none doth gain.
Sir Walter Raleigh *(c.1552-1618), English adventurer*

LOVE IS BLIND

If Jack's in love, he's no judge of Jill's beauty.
Benjamin Franklin *(1706-1790), American scientist and politician*

Many a man has fallen in love with a girl in a light so
dim he would not have chosen a suit by it.
Maurice Chevalier *(1888-1972), French singer and actor*

LOVE LETTERS

Be so good as to tell me . . . who is against my having
any shirts. You can deny clean linen to the inmates of a
hospital; but I do not intend to go without it. How your
meanness, that of your origin and that of your parents,
shines forth in your every act! My dove, the day I so far
forgot what I was that I could be willing to sell you
what I am, it may have been to get you under the covers
– but it wasn't to go uncovered.
Marquis de Sade *to his wife*

I will marry you so gladly with the old marriage service:
for better or worse, in sickness and in health, and
forsaking all others – until death do us part, Ha! – Ha!
Dorothy Thompson *to her intended, Sinclair Lewis*

My life was better before I knew you.
Edith Wharton to Morton Fullerton

I am so anxious for you not to abdicate and I think the
fact that you do is going to put me in the wrong light to
the entire world because they will say that I could have
prevented it.
Wallis Warfield Simpson to King Edward VIII

Please bring my flute.
Percy Bysshe Shelley to his wife, informing her that he had eloped
with Mary Godwin and asking her to join them

I hope you have lost your good looks, for while they
last any fool can adore you, and the adoration of fools
is bad for the soul. No, give me a ruined complexion
and a lost figure and sixteen chins on a farmyard of
Crow's feet and an obvious wig. Then you shall see me
coming out strong.
George Bernard Shaw to Mrs Patrick Campbell, an actress with
whom he had an amusing correspondence

I love the bitch to death.
Keith Richards on his wife

Darling Laura, sweet whiskers, do try to write me better
letters. Your last, dated 19 December received today, so
eagerly expected, was a bitter disappointment. Do
realise that a letter need not be a bald chronicle of
events; I know you lead a dull life now, my heart bleeds
for it, though I believe you could make it more
interesting if you had the will. But that is no reason to
make your letters as dull as your life. I simply am not
interested in Bridget's children, do grasp that.
Evelyn Waugh to his wife

Dear United States Army:
My husband asked me to write a recommend that he
supports his family. He cannot read, so don't tell him.
Just take him. He ain't no good to me. He ain't done
nothing but raise hell and drink lemon essence since I
married him eight years ago, and I got to feed seven
kids of his. Maybe you can get him to carry a gun. He's
good on squirrels and eating. Take him and welcome. I
need the grub and his bed for the kids. Don't tell him
this, but just take him.
*Anonymous letter hand-delivered in 1943 by an Arkansas man to
his draft board*

Loving you is like loving a red-hot poker which is a
worse bedfellow than even Lytton's umbrella; every
caress brings on agony.
Bertrand Russell to Ottoline Morrell

I could not love thee, dear, so much if I did not love my
freedom more.
*Johannes Brahms (1833-97), German composer, pianist and
conductor, to Agatha Von Siebold, breaking their engagement*

You must make a serious effort to change, my dear
Clara . . . passions are not a natural adjunct to human
nature, they are always exceptional or aberrant . . . look
on yourself as ill, dear Clara, seriously ill.
Johannes Brahms to Clara Schumann (1819-96), German pianist

If we love we must not live as other men and women
do. I cannot brook the wolfsbane of fashion and
foppery and tattle. You must be mine to die upon the
rack if I want you . . . Goodbye! I kiss you – o the
torments!
John Keats (1795-1821), English poet, to Fanny Brawne

Almost everything you have asked for – with the
exception of a mink coat – I have given you. But you
show no appreciation – only boredom, discontent. You
can't bear to remain at home of an evening. If you do, it
is only to cut your toe nails.
Henry Miller to his fifth wife

I will not meet you at the pier, as it will probably be
chilly.
*Anton Chekhov (1860-1904), Russian dramatist and writer, to
Olga Knipper*

LOVERS

I wouldn't give up one minute of my time with Richard
Burton . . . We were like magnets, alternating pulling
towards each other and inexorably pushing away.
Elizabeth Taylor

All mankind loves a lover.
*Ralph Waldo Emerson (1803-92), American poet and essayist,
Love, c.1840*

I doubt a girl would ever be satisfied with her lover's mind if she knew the whole of it.
Anthony Trollope *(1815-82), British novelist, The Small House at Allington, 1864*

'Tis strange what a man may do, and a woman yet think him an angel.
William Makepeace Thackery *(1811-63), British novelist*

I haven't had sex with enough Americans to generalise. You'd have to have sex with somebody from every state, and the last time I checked, I've missed North and South Dakota, Maine and Alaska. I did screw an Eskimo once, but she wasn't an American citizen. Ever try to make love in a kayak?
Lewis Grizzard, *American columnist, on being asked if Americans were good lovers*

Here is a sad slaughter at Windsor, the young men taking your leaves and going to France, and, although they are none of my lovers, yet I am loath to part with the men.
Nell Gwynn *(1650-87), actress and mistress of King Charles II in a letter to Madam Jennings, 1684*

All really great lovers are articulate, and verbal seduction is the surest road to actual seduction.
Marya Mannes

L U S T

License my roving hands, and let them go
Before, behind, between, above, below.
John Donne

All witchcraft comes from carnal lust which, in women, is insatiable.
Jacob Sprenger and **Hendrich Kramer,** *German Dominican monks, 1489*

Females are naturally libidinous, incite the males to copulation, and cry out during the act of coition.
Aristotle *(384-322BC),* Historia Animalium

To leap into a great vessel of cold water, or to put nettles in the codpiece.
Andrew Borde, *describing a cure for lust*

I've always been interested in lust, and everybody has
lusted for someone at some time in their lives. It's
human nature. The fact is, whether they acted it out or
not, there's a carnal chemical reaction that's fascinating
– especially if someone acted on it and then lost control
of their life after their animal side took over.
Michael Douglas, talking about his passionate film roles

It is very Victorian of the council to think that the ladies
of Darlington will lose control at the sight of a few male
bodies.
*Rita Fishwick, Mayor of Darlington, on a decision to ban a male
strip show*

No, not too old at fifty-three
a worn defeated fool like me.
Still the tickling lust devours
long stretches of my waking hours.
Busty girls in flowered scanties
hitching down St Michael panties.
Easing off their wet-look boots,
to step into their birthday suits.
Wicksteed, in Habeas Corpus *by Alan Bennett, 1973*

Thunder and lightning, wars, fires, plagues, have not
done that mischief to mankind as this burning lust.
Robert Burton (1577-1640), English philosopher, Anatomy of
Melancholy, *1621*

It is even possible, quite often, to spot women on the
pill from a certain deadness about their flesh, lustiness
about their eyes and lifelessness in their movements.
*Malcolm Muggeridge, British critic, speaking on BBC television,
1965*

They are much more amorous than men, and as
sparrows do not live long, because they are too hot and
too susceptible to love, so women last less time; because
they have a devouring heat, that consumes them by
degrees.
*Dr Nicholas de Venette explaining why women have a shorter life
expectancy than men*

Dancing is the perpendicular expression of a horizontal
desire.
Anon

MARRIAGE

It destroys one's nerves to be amiable every day to the same human being.
Benjamin Disraeli (1804-81), *former Conservative prime minister of Britain*

Don't marry a man to reform him – that's what reform schools are for.
Mae West

It is a truth universally acknowledged, that a single man in possession of a good fortune, must be in want of a wife.
Jane Austen

It's a funny thing that when a man hasn't anything on earth to worry about, he goes off and gets married.
Robert Frost

Someone asked me why women don't gamble as much as men do, and I gave the commonsensical reply that we don't have as much money. That was a true and incomplete answer. In fact, women's total instinct for gambling is satisfied by marriage.
Gloria Steinem

Putting one's hand into a bag of snakes on the chance of drawing out an eel.
Leonardo da Vinci (1452-1519), *Italian painter, sculptor, architect, engineer and scientist*

Nobody else could sleep with Dick. He wakes up during the night, switches on the lights, speaks into his tape recorder, or takes notes – it's impossible.
Pat Nixon, *wife of the former American president, Richard Nixon*

A man can be a fool and not know it – but not if he is married.
H. L. Mencken

Marriage is a bribe to make the housekeeper think she's a householder.
Thornton Wilder

One wishes marriage for one's daughter and, for one's descendants, better luck.
Fay Weldon

Marriage is an adventure, like going to war.
G. K. Chesterton (1874-1936), *British novelist and poet*

No married man is genuinely happy if he has to drink
worse whisky than he used to drink when he was single.
H. L. Mencken

I hate to be a failure. I hate and regret the failure of my
marriages. I would gladly give all my millions for just
one lasting marital success.
J. Paul Getty

Marriage is an alliance entered into by a man who can't
sleep with the window shut, and a woman who can't
sleep with the window open.
George Bernard Shaw

Marriage, a market which has nothing free but the
entrance.
Michel de Montaigne (1533-92), *French writer*

The chief cause of unhappiness in married life is that
people think that marriage is sex attraction which takes
the form of promises and hopes and happiness – a view
supported by public opinion and by literature. But
marriage cannot cause happiness. Instead, it is always
torture, which man has to pay for satisfying his sex
urge.
Leo Tolstoy (1828-1910), *Russian novelist*

He married a woman to stop her getting away.
Now she's there all day.
Philip Larkin (1922-85), *English poet*

Spouses are impediments to great enterprises.
Sir Francis Bacon

By all means marry; if you get a good wife, you'll be
happy. If you get a bad one, you'll become a
philosopher.
Socrates

If you are afraid of loneliness, do not marry.
Chekhov

If they only married when they fell in love, most people
would die unwed.
Robert Louis Stevenson

Politics doesn't make strange bedfellows – marriage does.
Groucho Marx

Most of the time in married life is taken up by talk.
Friedrich Nietzsche

No man is regular in his attendance at the House of Commons until he is married.
Benjamin Disraeli

In olden times sacrifices were made at the altar – a practice which is still continued.
Helen Rowland

My Nellie knows that the front door to the back is hers, and the outside world's mine. She's even quite good at changing plugs and all those little things you have to train women to do.
Lord Gormley, President of the National Union of Mineworkers, on his wife.

Bad enough to make mistakes, without going ahead and marrying them.
Craig Rice (1908-57), American novelist

You, poor and obscure, and small and plain as you are – I entreat you to accept me as a husband.
Mr Rochester in Jane Eyre *by Charlotte Brontë*

I've married a few people I shouldn't have, but haven't we all?
Mamie Van Doren, American actress

Do you take sugar?
Sir Ian MacGregor, former Chairman of the National Coal Board, to his wife – despite having being married to her for 45 years

It is true that I never should have married, but I didn't want to live without a man. Brought up to respect the conventions, love had to end in marriage. I'm afraid it did.
Bette Davis

I always say a girl must get married for love – and keep on getting married until she finds it.
Zsa Zsa Gabor, who is currently on her eighth marriage

He's the kind of man a woman would have to marry to get rid of.
Mae West

The only solid and lasting peace between a man and his wife is doubtless a separation.
Lord Chesterfield (1694-1773)

Marriage is not a word but a sentence.
Anon

My mother-in-law broke up my marriage. One day my wife came home early from work and found us in bed together.
Lenny Bruce (1926-66)

Marry money.
Max Schulman's advice to aspiring authors

An optimist is one who believes marriage is a gamble.
Laurence J. Peter

A working girl is one who quit her job to get married.
E. J. Kiefer

A man marries to have a home, but also because he doesn't want to be bothered with sex and all that sort of thing.
W. Somerset Maugham

Marriage is a mistake every man should make.
George Jessel

Dora and I are married, but just as happy as we were before.
Bertrand Russell

All marriages are happy. It's the living together afterward that causes all the trouble.
Raymond Hull

Matrimony is a process by which a grocer acquires an account the florist had.
Francis Rodman

One was never married, and that's his hell; another is, and that's his plague.
Robert Burton (1577-1640)

I shall marry in haste and repent at leisure.
James Branch Cabell

Marriage is a feast where the grace is sometimes better than the dinner.
Charles Caleb Colton (1780-1832)

Marriage is a community consisting of a master, a mistress, and two slaves – making in all two.
Ambrose Bierce

Marriage is the deep, deep peace of the double bed after the hurly-burly of the *chaise longue*.
Mrs Patrick Campbell

God, for two people to be able to live together for the rest of their lives is almost unnatural.
Jane Fonda

Happiness in marriage is entirely a matter of chance.
Jane Austen

Marriage is a bargain, and somebody has to get the worst end of the bargain.
Helen Rowland

Any intelligent woman who reads the marriage contract, and then goes into it, deserves all the consequences.
Isadora Duncan

It is always incomprehensible to a man that a woman should refuse an offer of marriage.
Jane Austen

Love-matches are made by people who are content, for a month of honey, to condemn themselves to a life of vinegar.
Countess of Blessington

People who haven't spoken to each other for years are on speaking terms again today – including the bride and groom.
Dorothy Parker, on marrying Alan Campbell for the second time

When you see what some girls marry, you realise how they must hate to work for a living.
Helen Rowland

When a girl marries, she exchanges the attentions of many men for the inattention of one.
Helen Rowland

Almost all married people fight, although many are ashamed to admit it. Actually, a marriage in which no quarrelling at all takes place may well be one that is dead or dying from emotional undernourishment. If you care, you probably fight.
Flora Davis

A man in love is incomplete until he has married. Then he's finished.
Zsa Zsa Gabor

Marriage always demands the greatest understanding of the art of insincerity possible between two human beings.
Vicki Baum

Marriage is a great institution, but I'm not ready for an institution.
Mae West

It was so cold I almost got married.
Shelley Winters

I married beneath me. All women do.
Nancy, Lady Astor

Before marriage, a man declares that he would lay down his life for you; after marriage, he won't even lay down his newspaper to talk to you.
Helen Rowland

Intelligent women always marry fools.
Anatole France

Marrying a man is like buying something you've been admiring for a long time in a shop window. You may love it when you get it home, but it doesn't always go with everything else in the house.
Jean Kerr

I'd marry again if I found a man who had $15 million and would sign over half of it to me before the marriage, and guarantee he'd be dead within the year.
Bette Davis

A book of which the first chapter is written in poetry and the remaining chapters in prose.
Beverly Nichols

I feel sure that no girl could go to the altar, and would probably refuse, if she knew all . . .
Queen Victoria

Writing is like getting married. One should never commit oneself until one is amazed at one's luck.
Iris Murdoch

In no country, I believe, are the marriage laws so iniquitous as in England, and the conjugal relation, in consequence, so impaired.
Harriet Martineau (1802-76), *British writer,* Society in America

The early marriages of silly children . . . where . . . every woman is married before she well knows how serious a matter human life is.
Harriet Martineau, Society in America

Each coming together of man and wife, even if they have been mated for many years, should be a fresh adventure; each winning should necessitate a fresh wooing.
Marie Stopes (1880-1958), *Scottish writer and birth-control campaigner,* Married Love, *1918*

Why should marriage bring only tears? All I wanted was a man with a single heart and we would stay together as our hair turned white, not somebody always after wriggling fish with his big bamboo rod.
Chuo Wen-Chun (c. *second century* BC), *Chinese poet*

Courtship is to marriage as a very witty prologue is to a very dull play.
William Congreve (1670-1729), The Old Bachelor, *1693*

Remember it is as easy to marry a rich woman
as a poor woman.
William Makepeace Thackeray, Pendennis, *1848*

No man should marry until he has studied anatomy and dissected at least one woman.
Honoré de Balzac (1799-1850), *French novelist,* La Physiologie du Marriage

The most happy marriage I can picture or imagine to myself would be the union of a deaf man to a blind woman.
Samuel Taylor Coleridge (1772-1834), *British poet*

Lastly (and this is, perhaps, the golden rule), no woman should marry a teetotaller, or a man who does not smoke.
Robert Louis Stevenson

If I had my choice, I would marry Roger Moore but have Sean Connery as my lover. He has a cross between menace and humour in his eyes. And a very chewable bottom lip.
Lois Maxwell, *British actress who played Miss Moneypenny in the James Bond films*

Never feel remorse for what you have thought about your wife; she has thought much worse things about you.
Jean Rostand *(1894-1977), French biologist and writer,* Le Mariage, *1927*

You can measure the social caste of a person by the distance between the husband's and wife's apartments.
King Alfonso XIII *of Spain (1886-1941)*

Marriage is a wonderful invention, but then again so is a bicycle repair kit.
Billy Connolly, *Scottish comedian*

The triumph of hope over experience.
Dr Samuel Johnson, *on the hasty remarriage of a friend after the death of his first wife, with whom he had been very unhappy*

Marrying merely to be married, to manage her own affairs, and have her own way – so childish! – or marrying merely to get an establishment – so base! How women, and such young creatures, can bring themselves to make these venal matches.
Maria Edeworth *(1767-1849), Irish novelist and essayist,* Ormond, *1817*

Every woman should marry – and no man.
Benjamin Disraeli, Lothian, *1870*

Marriage is far and away the most sanitary and least harmful of all the impossible forms of the man-woman relationship, though I would sooner jump off the Brooklyn Bridge than be married.
H. L. Mencken

A word which should be pronounced 'mirage'.
Herbert Spencer

Why did he not marry? Could the answer be that Jesus was not by nature the marrying sort?
Hugh Montefiore, *when Vicar of St Mary's, Cambridge*

I totally disagree with you. By any other arrangement four people would have been unhappy instead of two.
Alfred, Lord Tennyson, *in reply to the statement that the marriage of Jane and Thomas Carlyle had been a mistake. It had been suggested that with anyone but each other they might have been perfectly happy*

We sleep in separate rooms, we have dinner apart, we take separate vacations – we're doing everything we can to keep our marriage together.
Rodney Dangerfield

If I ever marry, it will be on a sudden impulse – as a man shoots himself.
H. L. Mencken

Zsa Zsa Gabor got married as a one-off and it was so successful she turned it into a series.
Bob Hope

Wife: Mr Watt next door blows his wife a kiss every morning as he leaves the house. I wish you'd do that.
Husband: But I hardly know the woman.
Alfred McFote

Some people ask the secret of our long marriage. We take time to do to a restaurant two times a week. A little candlelight dinner, soft music and dancing. She goes Tuesdays, I go Fridays.
Henny Youngman

I belong to Bridegrooms Anonymous. Whenever I feel like getting married, they send over a lady in a house coat and hair curlers to burn my toast for me.
Dick Marlin, *quoted in* Playboy *magazine, 1969*

She was another of his near Mrs.
Alfred McFote

The other night I said to my wife Ruth: 'Do you feel that the sex and excitement has gone out of our marriage?' Ruth said: 'I'll discuss it with you during the next commercial.'
Milton Berle, Variety

The whole point of marriage is to stop you getting anywhere near real life. You think it's a great struggle with the mystery of being. It's more like . . . being smothered in warm cocoa. There's sex, but it's not what you think. Marvellous for the first fortnight. Then every Wednesday, if there isn't a good late night concert on the third. Meanwhile you become a biological functionary, an agent of the great female womb, spawning away, dumping its goods on your lap for succour: Daddy, Daddy, we're here and we're expensive.
Malcolm Bradbury, Love on a Gunboat

EXCUSE ME COULD YOU PLEASE SAY THAT AGAIN I DON'T BELIEVE I HEARD YOU CORRECTLY LISTEN JUST WHO THE HELL DO YOU THINK YOU ARE FOR GOD'S SAKE WHAT AM I SUPPOSED TO BE YOUR SERVANT DON'T YOU DARE TALK TO ME IN THAT TONE OF VOICE I GUESS WE JUST AREN'T MEANT TO BE TOGETHER THAT'S ALL I'VE HAD IT UP TO HERE WITH YOU THAT'S RIGHT YOU HEARD ME THAT'S NOT MEANT TO BE A THREAT WE'RE JUST IN DIFFERENT TIMES IN OUR LIFE O.K. GO AHEAD THEN LEAVE I'LL HELP YOU PACK YOUR BAGS I GUESS I DON'T HAVE TO STAND.
Dan Greenberg and Suzanne O'Malley's wall paper design for the marital bedroom, How to Survive Love and Marriage, 1983

I never knew what real happiness was until I got married. And by then it was too late.
Max Kauffmann

There is nothing in the world like the devotion of a married woman. It's a thing no married man knows anything about.
Oscar Wilde, Lady Windermere's Fan, 1892

The first part of our marriage was very happy. But then, on the way back from the ceremony . . .
Henny Youngman

There were one hundred and seventeen psychoanalysts on the Pan Am flight to Vienna and I'd been treated by at least six of them, and married a seventh.
Erica Jong, Fear of Flying, 1973

Marriage is not just spirited communion and passionate embraces; marriage is also three meals a day and remembering to carry out the trash.
Joyce Brothers, *American psychologist*, Good Housekeeping, 1972

Marriage, I am convinced, is going to be the last subject
to be effectively computerised.
Drusilla Beyfus, author and journalist

When a woman gets married it is like jumping into a
hole in the ice in the middle of winter: you do it once
and you remember it the rest of your days.
Maxim Gorky (1876-1950), Russian writer, The Lower Depths,
1903

It has been discovered experimentally that you can
draw laughter from an audience anywhere in the world,
of any class or race, simply by walking on to a stage
and uttering the words: 'I am a married man'.
Ted Kavangh (1892-1958), British radio scriptwriter, New
Review, *1947*

'We stay together, but we distrust one another.'
'Ah, yes . . . but isn't that a definition of marriage?'
Malcolm Bradbury, British academic and novelist, The History
Man, *1975*

If you do not consent to be awakened your husband
will be deeply disappointed . . . He will not call it purity,
he will call it prudery; and he will be right . . . He will
know that you have not fully given yourself in
marriage: and married joys are for those who give with
royal generosity.
Reverend Gray's Introduction to the The Sex Fact *by Dr Helena
Wright, 1930*

Married women are kept women, and they are
beginning to find it out.
Logan Pearsall Smith (1865-1946), writer, Other People, *1931*

The incentive for girls to equip themselves for marriage
and home-making is genetic.
Kathleen Ollerenshaw, British educationalist, Education for Girls,
1961

He that get a wench with child and marry her
afterwards is as if a man should shit in his hat and then
clap it on his head.
Samuel Pepys (1633-1703), English diarist

MASTURBATION

A woman occasionally is quite a serviceable substitute for masturbation.
Karl Kraus

A niggling feeling of discomfort and unease follows masturbation, even in those who do not feel guilty about it.
Dr Charlotte Wolff, German psychologist, Love Between Women

Don't knock it, it's sex with someone you love.
Woody Allen

Masturbation the primary sexual activity of mankind. In the nineteenth century it was a disease; in the twentieth, it's a cure.
Thomas Szasz, American psychiatrist

Writers are the most masturbatory of creatures. Ask any writer – they're like monkeys.
Anthony Burgess, writer, talking on BBC Radio Four

MATING RITUAL

Four tested opening lines, Playboy *magazine, 1969*
• I don't believe we've met. I'm Mr Right.
• If National Security were at stake, would you spend the night with a man whose name you don't even know?
• I'm glad you don't recognise me. I'd rather have you like me for myself.
• I don't dance. But I'd love to hold you while you do.

Roseberry to his lady says, 'My Hinnie and my succour, O shall we do the thing ye ken, or shall we take our supper?'
     Wi' modest face, sae fu' o' grace, replied the bonny lady; 'My noble Lord do as you please, but supper is na ready.'
Anon (quoted by Burns in The Merry Muses of Caledonia)

MEN

A man is by nature a sexual animal. I've always had my special pets.
Mae West

Men are but children, too, though they have grey hairs;
they are only a larger size.
Seneca *(c. 4 BC-AD 65), Roman playwright and author*

Male sexual response is far brisker and more automatic.
It is triggered easily by things – like putting a quarter in
a vending machine.
Dr Alex Comfort

A man running after a hat is not half so ridiculous as a
man running after a woman.
G. K. Chesterton

If man is only a little lower than the angels, the angels
should reform.
Mary Wilson Little

There's nineteen men livin' in my neighbourhood,
eighteen of them are fools and the one ain't no doggone
good.
Bessie Smith

It's a man's world and you men can have it.
Katherine Ann Porter *(1890-1980), American writer*

The only really masterful noise a man ever makes in a
house is the noise of his key, when he is still on the
landing, fumbling for the lock.
Colette

His mother should have thrown him away and kept the
stork.
Mae West

A man's home may seem to be his castle on the outside;
inside, it is more often his nursery.
Clare Boothe Luce *(1903-87), American journalist, playwright
and politician*

If men had more up top we'd need less up front.
Jaci Stephen

The natural thing is to grab hold of someone and go
wallop! That's what we've been born to, us blokes.
Ian Dury, *British rock musician*

There are two things no man will admit he can't do
well: drive and make love.
Stirling Moss, *British racing driver, 1963*

All men are rapists. They rape us with their laws and
their codes.
Marilyn French, American author

I require only three things in a man: he must be
handsome, ruthless and stupid.
Dorothy Parker

Never accept rides from strange men, and remember
that all men are as strange as hell.
Robin Morgan

The male sex still constitutes in many ways the most
obstinate vested interests one can find.
Lord Longford

Men are beasts and even beasts don't behave as they do.
Brigitte Bardot

The more I see of men, the more I like dogs.
Madame de Staël (1766-1817), French writer

Giving a man space is like giving a dog a computer: the
chances are he will not use it wisely.
Bette-Jane Raphael

It's not the men in my life that count – it's the life in my
men.
Mae West

Give a man a free hand and he'll run it all over you.
Mae West

None of you [men] ask for anything – except
everything, but just for so long as you need it.
Doris Lessing

I'd never seen men hold each other. I thought the only
thing they were allowed to do was shake hands or fight.
Rita Mae Brown

I only like two kinds of men: domestic and imported.
Mae West

Probably the only place where a man can feel really
secure is in a maximum security prison, except for the
imminent threat of release.
Germaine Greer

I love men like some people like good food or wine.
Germaine Greer

The first time you buy a house you see how pretty the
paint is and buy it. The second time you look to see if
the basement has termites. It's the same with men.
Lupe Velez

I want a man who's kind and understanding. Is that too
much to ask of a millionaire?
Zsa Zsa Gabor

The male sex, as a sex, does not universally appeal to
me. I find the men today less manly; but a woman of
my age is not in a position to know exactly how manly
they are.
Katherine Hepburn

A man in the house is worth two in the street.
Mae West

I like men to behave like men – strong and childish.
Françoise Sagan, French novelist

I did not sleep; I never do when I am over happy, over
unhappy, or in bed with a strange man.
Edna O'Brien, The Love Nest, 1963

To a smart girl, men are no problem – they're the
answer.
Zsa Zsa Gabor

He's the kind of bore who's here today and here
tomorrow.
Binnie Barnes

Sometimes I think if there was a third sex men wouldn't
get so much as a second glance from me.
Amanda Vail (1921-66), American writer

The rule in the women's colleges was that after 7 p.m.
all men were beasts. Up until 7 p.m. they were all
angels, and the girls simply had to learn to live with that
routine and practise love in the afternoon.
Harry G. Johnson (1923-77) Cambridge in the 1950s

There are a lot of men who will ask me out just to be
with a celebrity.
Elizabeth Taylor

I truly believe I can be content only with a man who's a
little crazy.
Elizabeth Taylor, Elizabeth Takes Off

Happy is a man with a wife to tell him what to do and
a secretary to do it.
Lord Mancroft (1917-87), *British businessman and writer*

You know the problem with men? After the birth, we're
irrelevant.
Dustin Hoffman, *American actor*

However much men say sex is not on their minds all the
time, it is – most of the time.
Jackie Collins

American men are all mixed up today . . . There was a
time when this was a nation of Ernest Hemingways,
real men. The kind of men who could defoliate an
entire forest to make a breakfast fire – and then wipe
out an endangered species while hunting for lunch. But
not anymore. We've become a nation of wimps.
Pansies. Alan Alda types who cook and clean and
'relate' to their wives. Phil Donahue clones who are
'sensitive' and 'vulnerable' and understanding of their
children. And where's it gotten us? I'll tell you where.
The Japanese make better cars. The Israelis better
soldiers. And the rest of the world is using our
embassies for target practice.
Bruce Feirstein, Real Men Don't Eat Quiche, Playboy *magazine*,
1982

It's no news to anyone that nice guys finish last. Almost
every female I know has had the uncomfortable
experience of going out with the 'nice man', spelled,
'N-E-R-D'. How many times has your girlfriend said,
'He's so sweet and so cute, so why don't I like him?'
Let's face it, when an attractive but aloof ('cool') man
comes along, there are some of us who offer to shine his
shoes with our underpants. If he has a mean streak,
somehow this is 'attractive'. There are thousands of
scientific concepts as to why this is so, and yes, yes, it's
very sick – but none of this helps.
Lynda Barry, Big Ideas *cartoon*, 1987

No nice men are good at getting taxis.
Katherine Whitehorn, *the* Observer, 1977

There is nothing about which men lie so much as their sexual powers. In this at least every man is, what in his heart he would like to be, a Casanova.
W. Somerset Maugham, A Writer's Notebook, *1941*

Is it too much to ask that women be spared the daily struggle for superhuman beauty in order to offer it to the caresses of a subhumanly ugly mate?
Germaine Greer, The Female Eunuch, *1970*

On such a basis, one can't call a man ugly.
Caroline (La Belle) Otero (1868-1965), actress, on receiving a priceless jewel from a hideous lover

He must be a creature who makes me feel that I am a woman.
Elinor Glyn (1865-1943), novelist, giving her definition of a man

Men are like wine – some turn to vinegar, but the best improve with age.
Pope John XXIII quoted in Thoughts in a Dry Season *by Gerald Brenan, 1978*

About sex especially men are born unbalanced; we might almost say men are born mad. They scarcely reach sanity till they reach sanctity.
G. K. Chesterton

Whenever I date a guy, I think, is this the man I want my children to spend their weekends with?
Rita Rudner

Women want mediocre men, and men are working to be as mediocre as possible.
Margaret Mead

Some of my best leading men have been horses and gods.
Elizabeth Taylor

Men are creatures with two legs and eight hands.
Jayne Mansfield (1933-1967), American actress

I never hated a man enough to give him his diamonds back.
Zsa Zsa Gabor

One hell of an outlay for a very small return with most of them.
Glenda Jackson, British actress and politician

MEN AND WOMEN

The sad lesson in life is that you treat a girl like that
with respect, and the next guy comes along and he's
banging the hell out of her.
Art Buchwald

Men play the game; women know the score.
Roger Woddis

I judge how much a man cares for a woman by the
space he allots her under a jointly shared umbrella.
Jimmy Cannon

The most interesting woman characters in a picture are
whores, and every man in love is a sex pervert at heart.
Billy Wilder, American film director

Men want a woman whom they can turn on and off
like a light switch.
Ian Fleming

If a woman wants to hold a man, she has merely to
appeal to the worst of him.
Oscar Wilde, Lady Windermere's Fan

A man who is honest with himself wants a woman to
be soft and feminine, careful of what she's saying and
talk like a man.
Ann-Margret, American actress

Boy meets girl, girl gets boy into pickle; boy gets pickle
into girl.
Jack Woodford (1894-1971)

Men look at themselves in mirrors. Women look for
themselves.
Elissa Melamed

The average man is more interested in a woman who is
interested in him than he is in a woman with beautiful
legs.
Marlene Dietrich

A man's heart may have a secret sanctuary where only
one woman may enter, but it is full of little anterooms
which are seldom vacant.
Helen Rowland

A man thinks he knows, but a woman knows better.
Chinese proverb

Plain women know more about men than beautiful
ones do.
Katherine Hepburn

Men have been trained and conditioned by women, not
unlike the way Pavlov conditioned his dogs, into
becoming their slaves. As compensation for their
labours men are given periodic use of a woman's
vagina.
Esther Vilar

Woman serves as a looking-glass possessing the magic
powers of reflecting the figure of man at twice its
natural size.
Virginia Woolf

A woman is a woman until the day she dies, but a
man's a man only as long as he can.
Moms Mabley

I don't mind living in a man's world as long as I can be
a woman in it.
Marilyn Monroe

Why does a woman work ten years to change a man's
habits and then complain that he's not the man she
married?
Barbra Streisand

Men always fall for frigid women because they put on
the best show.
Fanny Brice

A woman has to be twice as good as a man to go half as
far.
Fannie Hurst

Women prefer men who have something tender about
them – especially the legal kind.
Kay Ingram

Whether women are better than men I cannot say – but
I can say they are certainly no worse.
Golda Meir

A romantic man often feels more uplifted with two
women than with one; his love seems to hit the ideal
mark somewhere between the two different faces.
Elizabeth Bowen

Woman's life must be wrapped up in a man, and the cleverest woman on earth is the biggest fool with a man.
Dorothy Parker

Women have always been the guardians of wisdom and humanity which makes them natural, but usually secret rulers. The time has come for them to rule openly, but together with and not against men.
Dr Charlotte Wolff, German writer and psychologist, Bisexuality: A study

Girls are so queer you never know what they mean. They say no when they mean yes, and drive a man out of his wits for the fun of it.
Louisa May Alcott (1832-88), American author, Little Women

Men know that women are an overmatch for them, and therefore they choose the weakest or the most ignorant. If they did not think so, they never could be afraid of women knowing as much as themselves.
Dr Samuel Johnson

When Eve ate this particular apple, she became aware of her own womanhood, mentally. And mentally she began to experiment with it. She has been experimenting ever since. So has man. To the rage and horror of both of them.
D. H. Lawrence (1885-1930), English writer, Fantasia of the Unconscious

There is a vast difference between the savage and the civilised man, but it is never apparent to their wives until after breakfast.
Helen Rowland

The man who gets on best with women is the one who knows best how to get on without them.
Charles Baudelaire (1821-67), French poet

There are two things a real man likes – danger and play; and he likes woman because she is the most dangerous of playthings.
Friedrich Nietzsche

Most men who run down women are only running down a certain woman.
Remy de Gourmont (1858-1915), French critic and novelist

Women love men for their defects; if men have enough
of them women will forgive them everything, even their
gigantic intellects.
Oscar Wilde

More and more it appears that, biologically, men are
designed for short, brutal lives and women for long,
miserable ones.
Estell Ramey, Professor of Physiology, Georgetown University,
1985

Men have a much better time of it than women. For
one thing, they marry later; for another thing, they die
earlier.
H. L. Mencken

Men make gods, and women worship them.
*James G. Frazer (1854-1941), Scottish classicist and
anthropologist*

Sure men were born to lie, and women to believe them.
John Gay (1685-1732), English playwright

A man is as good as he has to be, and a woman as bad
as she dares.
Elbert Hubbard

Men lose more conquests by their own awkwardness
than by any virtue in the woman.
Ninon de Lenclos

Women represent the triumph of matter over mind, just
as men represent the triumph of mind over morals.
Oscar Wilde, The Picture of Dorian Gray, *1891*

It is rare that one can see in a little boy the promise of a
man, but one can almost always see in a little girl the
threat of a woman.
Alexandre Dumas (1824-95), French writer

All women become like their mothers. That is their
tragedy. No man does. That's his.
Oscar Wilde, The Importance of Being Earnest, *1895*

Women who love the same man have a kind of bitter
freemasonry.
Max Beerbohm

A woman can become a man's friend only in the
following stages – first an acquaintance, next a mistress,
and only then a friend.
Anton Chekhov (1860-1904), Russian dramatist, Uncle Vanya,
1897

We study ourselves three weeks, we love each other
three months, we squabble three years, we tolerate each
other thirty years, and then the children start all over
again.
Hippolyte Taine (1828-93), French critic and historian

She was so glad to see me go, that I have almost a mind
to come again, that she may again have the same
pleasure.
Dr Samuel Johnson

You see, dear, it is not true that woman was made from
man's rib; she was really made from his funny bone.
J. M. Barrie (1860-1937), What Every Woman Knows, 1908

While man has a sex, woman is a sex.
Elizabeth Belfort Bax

Men and women do not have the faintest idea of what
to do with one another. Each sex looks at the other
with suspicion. The slightest gesture (scratching an ear),
the most casual remark (how are your tomatoes?) are
seen as hostile acts. Now that women are equal, they
feel awful about it and wonder if they should have
pushed so hard. Men would like to reach out and help
but are afraid they will be smashed in the head.
Bruce Jay Friedman, 'Sex and the Lonely Guy', Esquire magazine,
1977

We can call each other girls, chicks, broads, birds and
dames with equanimity. Many of us prefer to do so
since the word 'woman', being two syllables, is long,
unwieldy and earnest. But a man must watch his ass.
Never may a man be permitted to call any female a
'chick'. He may call you a broad or a dame only if he is
a close friend and fond of John Garfield movies. The
term 'bird', generally used by fatuous Englishmen, is
always frowned upon.
Cynthia Heimel, American journalist and writer, Sex Tips for
Girls, 1983

The hardest task in a girl's life is to prove to a man that his intentions are serious.
Helen Rowland, Reflections of a Bachelor Girl, *1903*

The only place men want depth in a woman is in her decolletage.
Zsa Zsa Gabor *(attrib)*

God created man, and finding him not sufficiently alone, gave him a companion to make him feel his solitude more.
Paul Valéry *(1871-1945)*, Telquel *magazine, 1943*

There are three things a man can do with women: love them, suffer for them, or turn them into literature.
Stephen Stills, *Canadian rock star*

It is a mark of civilised men that they defend their women.
Taki, *British gossip columnist and author*, Spectator *magazine, 1980*

'What do you call a bad man?'
'The sort of man who admires innocence.'
'And a bad woman?'
'Oh, the sort of woman a man never gets tired of.'
Oscar Wilde, A Woman of No Importance

I am a woman meant for a man, but I never found a man who could compete.
Bette Davis, *speaking about her five marriages*

Men shall always be what the women make them; if, therefore, you would have men great and virtuous, impress upon the minds of women what greatness and virtues are.
Jean-Jacques Rousseau *(1712-78), French social philosopher and writer*

Since God chose his spouse from among women, most excellent Lady, because of your honour, not only should men refrain from reproaching women, but should also hold them in great reverence.
Christine de Pisan *(c.1363-1430) French author and poet*, La Vite des Dames, *1404*

Men, some to business, some to pleasure take;
But every woman is at heart a rake.
Alexander Pope *(1688-1744), British poet*, Moral Essays, *1732*

You men have more patience with the hen that
befouleth thy table but layeth a fresh egg daily, than
with thy wife when she bringeth forth a little girl.
Consider the fruit of the woman, and have patience; not
for every cause is it right to beat her.
Bernardino of Siena, Sermons, 1427

God made woman for the man, and for the good and
increase of the world.
Alfred, Lord Tennyson (1809-92), British poet, Edwin Morris,
1860

I would rather trust a woman's instinct than a man's
reason.
Stanley Baldwin (1867-1947), British statesman

When a man gives his opinion, he's a man. When a
woman gives her opinion, she's a bitch.
Bette Davis, attrib

Most men tell me that they prefer the woman to get out
of bed in the middle of the night so that they don't have
to look at her.
Soraya Khasoogi

M I S T R E S S E S

Music is my mistress and she plays second fiddle to no
one.
Duke Ellington

She sleeps with others because she loves them, but for
money, only with me!
Ferenc Molnar, Hungarian novelist, on being told that his mistress
had been unfaithful to him while he was out of town

Who is she? The executive mistress, that important
figure standing behind so many top executives and
kneeling in front of still more. A national survey
conducted by *Off the Wall Street Journal* shows that
86% of senior officers in 65% of the Fortune 500
companies keep a mistress currently, and have kept a
mistress in the past or intend to find one as soon as they
finish reading this article.
Off the Wall Street Journal, *1982*

My advice is to keep two mistresses. Few men have the stamina for more.
Ovid, Cures for Love

Next to the pleasures of taking a new mistress is that of being rid of an old one.
William Wycherley *(1640-1716)*, The Country Wife

My executive often arrives at the apartment exhausted and emotionally detached after a hard day of corporate manipulation and chancery, says Karen (not her real name). He depends on me to raise his lowered interest rate and stimulate his private sector.
Off the Wall Street Journal, *1982*

I have lost my mistress, horse and wife, and when I think of human life, Cry mercy 'twas no worse. My mistress sickly, poor and old, My wife damn'd ugly and a scold, I am sorry for my horse.
Anon

That shouldn't hamper your marrying.
Queen Caroline *(1683-1737), on her death-bed urging her husband King George II to marry again. He had replied that he would have mistresses*

When a man marries his mistress it creates a job opportunity.
Sir James Goldsmith

Buy Old Masters. They fetch a better price than old mistresses.
Lord Beaverbrook, Canadian press magnate

O sire, it were better to be your mistress than your wife.
Catherine Parr (1512-48), sixth wife of King Henry VIII

She is the only woman in France who makes me forget I am a sexagenarian.
King Louis XV (1741-93), on his mistress, Madame du Barry

I need several mistresses; if I had only one, she'd be dead inside eight days.
Alexandre Dumas

MODERN TIMES

In these days when royalties vanish, when children turn against their parents, when husbands turn on wives and uncles on nieces, one thing stands unshaken – the love of a woman for her gynaecologist.
A. Dickson Wright, British surgeon

Modern man isn't as virile as he used to be. Instead of making things happen, he waits for things to happen to him. He goes with the current. Something . . . has led him to stop swimming upstream.
Marcello Mastroianni, Italian actor, quoted in Playboy *magazine, 1965*

We have to compete with newspapers which have double-page spreads of pubic hair.
Rupert Murdoch, publisher of the Sun *and the* News of the World, *justifying pin-ups in his newspapers*

The so called 'new morality' is too often the old immorality condoned.
Lord Shawcross, British politician

Sex has become one of the most discussed subjects of modern times. The Victorians pretended it did not exist; the moderns pretend that nothing else exists.
Archbishop Fulton J. Sheen

MODESTY

I wasn't really naked. I simply didn't have any clothes
on.
Josephine Baker

In some remote regions of Islam it is said a woman
caught unveiled by a stranger will raise her skirt to
cover her face.
Raymond Mortimer (1895-1980), British literary critic and writer

Put off your shame with your clothes when you go in to
your husband, and put it on again when you come out.
Theano (c.420BC), Greek priestess

Age will bring all things, and everyone knows,
Madame, that twenty is no age to be a prude.
Molière (1622-73), French dramatist, Le Misanthrope, 1666

The perfect hostess will see to it that the works of male
and female authors be properly separated on her
bookshelves. Their proximity, unless they happen to be
married, should not be tolerated.
Lady Gough, Etiquette, 1836

She just wore enough for modesty – no more.
Robert Williams Buchanan (1841-1901), British poet and writer,
White Rose and Red, 1871

It serves me right for putting all my eggs in one bastard.
Dorothy Parker, on going to hospital to have an abortion

MONEY

When you don't have any money, the problem is food.
When you have money, it's sex. When you have both,
it's health. If everything is simply Jake, then you're
frightened of death.
J. P. Donleavy

No woman marries for money; they are all clever
enough, before marrying a millionaire, to fall in love
with him first.
Cesare Pavese (1908-50), Italian author

Money is the sinews of love, as of war.
George Farquhar (1678-1707), Irish dramatist

MORALS

Morality consists in suspecting other people of not being legally married.
George Bernard Shaw, The Doctor's Dilemma, 1906

We are told by moralists with the plainest faces that immorality will spoil our looks.
Logan Pearsal Smith (1865-1946), American essayist

Morality comes with the sad wisdom of age, when the sense of curiosity has withered.
Graham Greene (1904-91), British novelist

The Englishman thinks he is moral when he is only uncomfortable.
George Bernard Shaw, The Devil, Man and Superman

Morality is simply the attitude we adopt towards people we personally dislike.
Oscar Wilde

About morals, I know only that what is moral is what you feel good after and what is immoral is what you feel bad after.
Ernest Hemingway

I did not use paint, I made myself up morally.
Eleanora Duse (1859-1924), Italian actress, Le Gaulois, 1922

MOTHERS AND MOTHERHOOD

Motherhood is the most emotional experience of one's life. One joins a kind of women's mafia.
Janet Suzman, English actress

I'm not against mothers. I am against the ideology which expects every woman to have children, and I'm against the circumstances under which mothers have to have their children.
Simone de Beauvoir

It is neither necessary nor just to make it imperative on women that they should either be mothers or nothing, or that if they have been mothers they should be nothing else during the whole remainder of their lives.
Harriet Taylor

Devoted grandmother though I am now, I strongly
resent the assumption that our capacity for childbearing
and our natural inclination towards childcare and child-
rearing are the only reasons for our being here on earth.
Mary Stott

I always thought they'd become more independent as
they got older. But it doesn't work like that. I think that
all new mothers imagine their baby can't survive
without them, but in fact someone else can look after
the baby unless you're breast-feeding. It's when they get
older that the parents assume a more special role. Other
people can't really help with growing-up problems,
homework or giving your children the continuity and
stability they need in their lives.
Carol Barnes, ITN newsreader

If I was the Virgin Mary, I would have said no.
Stevie Smith (1902-71), British poet and novelist

Mothers are fonder than fathers of their children
because they are more certain they are their own.
Aristotle

Women who miscalculate are called mothers.
Abigail Van Buren

Instant availability without continuous presence is
probably the best role a mother can play.
Lotte Bailyn

MUSIC

Hearing in the distance
Two mandolins like creatures in the dark
Creating the agony of ecstasy.
George Barker (1913-91), British author and poet

Love is not the dying moan of a distant violin – it's the
triumphant twang of a bedspring.
S. J. Perelman (1904-79), American humorist

Music helps set a romantic mood. Some men believe the
only good music is live music. Imagine her surprise
when you say, 'I don't need a stereo – I have an
accordion!' Then imagine the sound of the door
slamming.
Martin Mull, quoted in Playboy magazine, 1978

When I first glimpse the backs of women's knees I seem
to hear the first movement of Beethoven's Pastoral
Symphony.
Anon

Seeing unhappiness in the marriage of friends, I was
content to have chosen music and laughter as a
substitute for a husband.
Elsa Maxwell (1883-1963), society hostess

MYTHS

Contemporary man has rationalised the myths, but he
has not been able to destroy them.
Octavio Paz, Mexican author and poet

I think women are basically quite lazy. Marriage is still
a woman's best investment, because she can con some
man into supporting her for the rest of her life.
Alan Whicker, British television broadcaster and writer, 1972

We consider first that the promiscuous assemblage of
the sexes in the same class is a dangerous innovation . . .
that the presence of young females as passive spectators
in the operating theatre is an outrage to our natural
instincts and feelings, and calculated to destroy those
sentiments of respect and admiration with which the
opposite sex is regarded by all right-minded men, such
feelings being a mark of civilisation and refinement.
Medical School committee, Middlesex Hospital, 1861

Were it not for gold and women, there would be no
damnation.
Cyril Tourneur (1575-1626), English dramatist, The Revenger's
Tragedy, *1607*

NUDITY

Nakedness reveals itself. Nudity is placed on display . . .
the nude is condemned to never being naked. Nudity is
a form of dress.
John Berger, British critic

I have seen three emperors in their nakedness and the
sight was not inspiring.
Prince Otto Von Bismarck (1815-98), Prussian statesman

Whew, what a bony butt.
Michael Douglas, on seeing himself naked on screen

Don't miss our show! Six beautiful dancing girls! Five beautiful costumes!
Poster outside a London nightclub

The trouble with nude dancing is that not everything stops when the music does.
Robert Helpmann, dancer and choreographer

I'm not *against* naked girls – not as often as I'd like to be.
Benny Hill

Full frontal nudity . . . has now become accepted by every branch of the theatrical profession with the possible exception of the lady accordion players.
Denis Norden, British humorist, You Can't Have Your Kayak and Heat It, *1973*

I didn't pay three pounds fifty just to see half a dozen acorns and a chipolata.
Noël Coward, after watching male nude scenes in David Storey's The Changing Room

Actually, nude bathing at seaside resorts is nothing new to this country, or at least certain parts of it.
Mr E. Bareham, Editor of British Naturism *magazine*

Scores of artistically selected teams of traditional dancers from various parts of Kenya exposed themselves to the world scouts delegates in a grand performance on Saturday night.
Daily Nation, quoted in Private Eye *magazine*

I'm an interesting, shy and vulnerable woman. My husband has never seen me naked. Nor has he expressed the least desire to do so.
Dame Edna Everege (aka Barry Humphries), housewife and superstar

To an artist a husband named Bicket
Said 'Turn your backside and I'll kick it.
You have painted my wife
in the nude to the life
Do you think for a moment that's cricket?'
Anon

People who live in glass houses should pull the blinds when removing their trousers.
Spike Milligan, British comedian, The Little Pot Boiler

It was nice to see your private parts anyway.
David Frost to Lord Montagu, who explained that part of his stately home was open to the public

If one wants to see people naked one doesn't go to the theatre, one goes to a Turkish bath.
Noël Coward, quoted in the Observer, *1971*

Oh yes, I had the radio on.
Marilyn Monroe, discussing a nude photograph of herself, with a journalist who asked, 'Didn't you have anything on?'

I think naked people are very nice. Posing in the nude is perhaps the best way of reaching people.
Stella Stevens, American actress, 1968

This is 'in the raw' theatre. There have been objections on moral grounds. But the main worry is hygiene. People fear AIDS. However, the nudists will be screened off from the rest of the audience and individual washable seat covers will be supplied.
Theatre spokesman for the Brewhouse Theatre, after there were protests when the management agreed that a group of nudists should be allowed to enjoy the play Steaming *stark naked*

O B E S I T Y

A big man has no time really to do anything but just sit and be big.
F. Scott Fitzgerald

O B S C E N I T Y

Obscenity is whatever happens to shock some elderly and ignorant magistrate.
Bertrand Russell, British philosopher, Look, *1954*

I just want to go and be obscene in private with my friends.
Richard Neville, Australian journalist, on his release after the OZ *magazine obscenity trial, 1971*

OPINIONS

A society in which women are taught anything but the management of a family, the care of men, and the creation of the future generation, is a society which is on the way out.
L. Ron Hubbard *(1911-86), American science-fiction writer and founder of the Church of Scientology*

Women should remain at home, sit still, keep house, and bring up children.
Martin Luther *(1483-1546), German founder of Protestantism*

ORGASM

Is there a way to accept the concept of the female orgasm and still command the respect of your foreign auto-mechanic?
Bruce Feirstein, *'Real Men Don't Eat Quiche'*, Playboy *magazine,1982*

I finally had an orgasm . . . and my doctor told me it was the wrong kind.
Woody Allen, Manhattan, *1979*

In the case of some women, orgasms take a bit of time. Before signing on with a partner, make sure you are willing to lay aside, say, the month of June, with sandwiches having to be bought in.
Bruce Jay Friedman

The orgasm has replaced the cross as the focus of longing and the image of fulfilment.
Malcolm Muggeridge

An orgasm is just a reflex like a sneeze.
Dr Ruth (Westheimer)

As women have known since the dawn of our time, the primary site for stimulation to orgasm centres on the clitoris. The revolution unleashed by the Kinsey Report of 1953 has, by now, made this information available to men who, for whatever reason, had not figured it out for themselves by the more obvious routes of experience and sensitivity.
Stephen Jay Gould, *American geologist and writer,* Bully for Brontosaurus, *1991*

When the ecstatic body grips its heaven, with little sobbing cries.
E. R. Doods (1893-1979), British classical scholar

The soil is fertile, Sir, because it is full of micro-orgasms.
Thirteen-year-old pupil at Cranleigh School

So female orgasm is simply a nervous climax to sex relations . . . It may be thought of as a sort of pleasure prize like a prize that comes with a box of cereal. It is all to the good if the prize is there but the cereal is valuable and nourishing if it is not.
Madeline Gray, American writer, The Normal Woman, *1967*

When modern woman discovered the orgasm it was (combined with modern birth control) perhaps the biggest single nail in the coffin of male dominance.
Eva Diges, English writer

ORGIES

You get a better class of person at orgies, because people have to keep in trim more. There is an awful lot of going round holding in your stomach, you know. Everybody is very polite to each other. The conversation isn't very good but you can't have everything.
Gore Vidal

Once, a philosopher; twice, a pervert!
Voltaire (1694-1778), French writer. After participating in an orgy and being invited back the very next night, Voltaire declined

If God meant us to have group sex, I guess he'd have given us all more organs.
Malcolm Bradbury, British author

PARENTS

They fuck you up your mum and dad
They may not mean to, but they do.
They fill you with the faults they had
and add some extra, just for you.
Philip Larkin, 'This Be The Verse', High Windows, *1974*

The first half of our lives is ruined by our parents, and the second half by our children.
Clarence Darrow (1857-1938), American lawyer

To lose one parent may be regarded as a misfortune: to lose both looks like carelessness.
Oscar Wilde, The Importance of Being Earnest, *1895*

The thing that impresses me most about America is the way parents obey their children.
Duke of Windsor

If you have never been hated by your child you have never been a parent.
Bette Davis

PASSIONS

Great passions don't exist, they are liar's fantasies. What do exist are little loves that may last for a short or longer while.
Anna Magnani (1918-1976), Italian actress

I've always admitted that I'm ruled by my passions.
Elizabeth Taylor

Men are often blind to the passions of women; but every woman is as quick-sighted as a hawk on these occasions.
Henry Fielding (1707-54), English novelist, Amelia, *1751*

The natural man has only two primal passions – to get and to beget.
Sir William Osler (1849-1919), Canadian physician

Be a good animal, true to your animal instincts.
D. H. Lawrence

Some people lose control of their sluice gates of passion.
The Beijing Workers Daily, *1981*

If we resist our passions, it is more because of their weakness than because of our strength.
François, duc de La Rochefoucauld

Passion, though a bad regulator, is a powerful spring.
Ralph Waldo Emerson (1803-82), American essayist, poet and philosopher

The passions are the only orators which always
persuade.
François, duc de La Rochefoucauld

A really grand passion is comparatively rare nowadays.
It is the privilege of people who have nothing to do.
That is the one use of the idle classes in the country.
Oscar Wilde, A Woman of No Importance, 1893

The passion and starry-eyed joys of the honeymoon are
but callow experiments in a search for the magnificent
which lies beyond the horizon.
Barbara Cartland, British romantic novelist

Nobody on earth loves more than I, because I love
without being ashamed of the reason why I love.
*George Sand (1804-76), French writer, and lover of the poet
Alfred de Musset and the composer Frédéric Chopin*

You had forgotten, then, that I loved you to distraction,
and that I was your husband? One or the other can
drive a man to extremities – how much more so the two
together.
Marie de La Fayette (1634-93), French writer, The Princess of
Cleves

We must act out passion before we can feel it.
Jean-Paul Sartre, French philosopher and writer, The Words,
1964

Why not put up that pane of glass called passion
between us? It may distort things at times, but it's
wonderfully convenient. But no, we were two of a kind,
allies and accomplices. In terms of grammar, I could not
become the object, or the subject. He had neither the
capacity nor the desire to define our roles in any such
way.
Françoise Sagan, French writer, A Certain Smile, 1956

PAST

If someone with whom one is having an affair keeps on
mentioning some woman whom he knew in the past,
however long ago it is since they separated, one is
always irritated.
Sei Shonagon (c.10th century), The Pillow Book of Sei Shonagon

PATERNITY

There was a young man in Rome that was very like
Augustus Caesar; Augustus took knowledge of it and
sent for the man, and asked him: 'Was your mother
ever at Rome?' He answered, 'No Sir; but my father
was.'
Francis Bacon (1561-1626)

He that bulls the cow must keep the calf.
16th-century proverb

Maternity is a matter of fact; paternity is a matter of
opinion.
Anon

PENIS

He is proud that he has the biggest brain of all the
primates, but he attempts to conceal that he also has the
biggest penis.
Desmond Morris

One night I was sitting with friends at a table in a
crowded Key West bar. At a nearby table, there was a
mildly drunk woman with a very drunk husband.
Presently, the woman approached us and asked me to
sign a paper napkin. All this seemed to anger her
husband; he staggered over to the table and, after
unzipping his trousers and hauling out his equipment,
said: 'Since you're autographing things, why don't you
autograph this?' The tables surrounding us had grown
silent, so a great many people heard my reply, which
was: 'I don't know if I can autograph it, but perhaps I
can initial it.'
Truman Capote

A man is two people, himself and his cock. A man
always takes his friend to the party. Of the two, the
friend is the nicer, being more able to show his feelings.
Beryl Bainbridge, English novelist

I wonder why men get serious at all. They have this
delicate, long thing hanging outside their bodies which
goes up and down by its own will. If I were a man I
would always be laughing at myself.
Yoko Ono

The penis is obviously going the way of the veriform appendix.
Jill Johnstone, *American writer*

He put it back into his pants as if he were folding a dead octopus tentacle into his shorts.
Richard Brautigan

During the feminist revolution, the battle lines were again simple. It was easy to tell the enemy, he was the one with the penis. This is no longer strictly true. Some men are okay now, we're allowed to like them again. We still have to keep them in line, of course, but we no longer have to shoot them on sight.
Cynthia Heimel, Sex Tips for Girls, 1983

When his cock wouldn't stand up he blew his head off. He sold himself a line of bullshit and he bought it.
Germaine Greer on Ernest Hemingway

No woman except for so-called 'deviants' seriously wishes to be male and have a penis. But most women would like to have the privileges and opportunities that go with it.
Eliana Gianini Belotti, *Italian feminist*, Little Girls, 1973

An erection at will is the moral equivalent of a valid credit card.
Dr Alex Comfort, *British sexologist, quoted in the* New York Times, 1978

An erection is a mysterious thing. There's always that fear, each time one goes, that you won't be seeing it again.
Kirk Douglas, *American actor, in his autobiography,* The Ragman's Son

Generally speaking, it is in love as it is in war, where the
longest weapon carries it.
John Leland, Fanny Hill

Keithley Miller (an American lady) asked a Scotsman
whether it was true that they wore nothing under their
kilts. Lifting up his kilt, the somewhat inebriated Scot
revealed all and asked: 'What do you think of that?' She
replied: 'Well, it looks like a penis only smaller.'
Anon

PLASTIC SURGERY

If you have a psychotic fixation and you go to the
doctor and you want these two fingers amputated, he
will not cut them off. But he will remove your genitals. I
have more trouble getting a prescription for valium
than I do having my uterus lowered and made into a
penis.
Lily Tomlin, American actress, quoted in Rolling Stone *magazine,*
1974

PLEASURE

Pleasure is the only thing to live for. Nothing ages like
happiness.
Oscar Wilde

You wear yourself out in the pursuit of wealth or love
or freedom, you do everything to gain some right, and
once it's gained, you take no pleasure in it.
Oriana Fallaci

All the things I really like to do are either immoral,
illegal or fattening.
Alexander Woollcott (1887-1943), American columnist and critic

If I had no duties, and no reference to futurity, I would
spend my life in driving briskly in a post-chaise with a
pretty woman.
Dr Samuel Johnson

Scratching is one of nature's sweetest gratifications, and
the one nearest at hand.
Michel de Montaigne (1533-92), French essayist

Going overseas? Emigration, business or lust pleasure.
Immediate passages available.
Misprint in the Liverpool Echo

Nine out of ten women would rather have a man who
would surreptitiously caress their thighs under a
nightclub table than a good, rugged chap who'll slap
them heartily on the back at a Saturday football game.
Marjorie Proops, British journalist and broadcaster

In diving to the bottom of pleasure we bring up more
gravel than pearls.
Honoré de Balzac

Men may experience an erection while on horseback, or
driving in a carriage or travelling by train; more rarely
perhaps while motoring or bicycling.
Van der Velde, Ideal Marriage

POLITICS

My choice in life was either to be a piano player in a
whorehouse or a politician. And to tell you the truth,
there's hardly any difference.
Harry S. Truman (1884-1972)

If presidents don't do it to their wives, they do it to the
country.
Mel Brooks

I still love you, but in politics there is no heart, only
head.
*Napolean Bonaparte (1769-1821), French Emperor, referring to
his divorce, for reasons of state, from the Empress Josephine, 1800*

PORNOGRAPHY

The worst that can be said about pornography is that it
leads not to anti-social acts but to the reading of more
pornography.
Gore Vidal, Reflections upon a Sinking Ship, 1969

It's red hot, mate. I hate to think of this sort of book
getting into the wrong hands. As soon as I've finished
this, I shall recommend they ban it.
Tony Hancock (1924-68), British comedian

The citizens' committee to clean up New York's porn-infested areas continued its series of rallies today, as a huge, throbbing, pulsating crowd sprang erect from nowhere and forced its way into the steaming nether regions surrounding the glistening, sweating intersection of Eighth Avenue and Forty-Second Street. Thrusting, driving, pushing its way into the usually receptive neighbourhood, the excited throng, now grown to five times its original size rammed itself again and again and again into the quivering, perspiring, musty dankness, fluctuating between eager anticipation and trembling revulsion. Now suddenly the tumescent crowd and the irresistible area were one heaving, alternately melting and thawing turgid entity, ascending to heights heretofore unexperienced. Then, with a gigantic, soul-searching, heart-stopping series of eruptions, it was over. Afterwards the crowd had a cigarette and went home.
'Weekend Update', Saturday Night Live, NBC TV

Immediately before dashing to the airport to fly home, the Prime Minister engaged in some personal and highly unorthodox garden party diplomacy. I did not see him myself but he is reported to have done some business behind a tree with General Gowon, the Nigerian Leader.
Report in the London Evening Standard

I would like to see all people who read pornography or have anything to do with it, put in a mental hospital for observation so we could find out what we have done to them.
Linda Lovelace, *American model and actress*

Obscenity is such a tiny kingdom that a single tour covers it completely.
Heywood Broun *(1888-1939), American journalist and novelist*

Pornography is the attempt to insult sex, to do dirt on it.
D. H. Lawrence

It'll be a sad day for sexual liberation when the pornography addict has to settle for the real thing.
Brendan Francis

Pornography is in the groin of the beholder.
Anon

Nine-tenths of the appeal of pornography is due to the indecent feelings concerning sex which moralists inculcate in the young; the other tenth is physiological, and will occur in one way or another, whatever the state of the law may be.
Bertrand Russell

The fact remains that, no matter how disturbing violent fantasies are, as long as they stay within the world of pornography they are still only fantasies. The man masturbating in a theatre showing a snuff film is still only watching a movie, not actually raping and murdering.
Deidre English, *American writer and editor*, Mother Jones, *1980*

She is the pin-up, the centrefold, the poster, the postcard, the dirty picture, naked, half-dressed, laid out, legs spread, breast or ass protruding. She is the thing she is supposed to be; the thing that makes him erect.
Andrea Dworkin, *American writer and journalist*, Pornography: Men Possessing Women, *1981*

Women, for centuries not having access to pornography and unable to bear looking . . . are astonished. Women do not believe that men believe what pornography says about women. But they do. From the worst to the best of them, they do.
Andrea Dworkin

A word about pornography. You'll need it. Lots of it
. . . The dirty, filthy degrading kind. But keep it *well hidden*. Don't discount secret wall panels, trick drawers, holes in the yard, etc. Especially if you have teenage boys or a Baptist wife with a housekeeping obsession. Also keep in mind that you could die at any moment and nothing puts a crimp in the funeral worse than having the bereaved family wonder what kind of sick, perverted beast you were under that kind and genteel exterior.
John Hughes, *'Very Married Sex'*, National Lampoon, *1979*

I got paid less for my pictures than the male photographers – it is the most sexually discriminating magazine of its kind. The editor is a man and many of the staff are male. They are imposing their values about what is sexy on to women.
Nikki Downey, *photographer*, For Women *magazine*

Pornography is any matter or thing exhibiting or
visually representing persons or animals performing the
sexual act whether normal or abnormal.
Ernst and Seagle, To the Pure, *1929*

Let's say, I think a man is more likely to make love to
his wife after coming to the revue bar than on any other
night of the year.
*Paul Raymond (Geoffrey Quinn), British magazine publisher,
1970*

Real pornography is movies starring Doris Day or any
picture of big-breasted girls to illustrate stories on lung
cancer.
Al Alvarez, British writer, 1968

P O W E R

The ultimate aphrodisiac.
Henry Kissinger

What the proprietorship of these papers is aiming at is
power, and power without responsibility, the
prerogative of the harlot through the ages.
*Stanley Baldwin (1867-1947), British Conservative politician and
Prime Minister, attacking the press barons at a by-election meeting
in 1931. Harold Macmillan, who was present, recalls his father-in-
law, the Duke of Devonshire, commenting: 'Good God, that's done
it. He's lost us the tarts' vote.'*

A man in love is like a sparrow caught with birdlime;
the more he struggles, the more he is entangled.
Madame de Staël (1766-1817), French writer

The men who really wield, retain, and covet power are
the kind who answer bedside phones while making
love.
Nicholas Pileggi

If you live with a man you must conquer him every day.
Otherwise he will go to another.
Brigitte Bardot

P R E G N A N C Y   A N D
P R O C R E A T I O N

If I had a cock for a day I would get myself pregnant.
Germaine Greer

If pregnancy were a book they would cut the last two chapters.
Nora Ephron

A hen is only an egg's way of making another egg.
Samuel Butler *(1835-1902), English author*

The act of procreation and the members employed therein are so repulsive, that if it were not for the beauty of the faces and the adornments of the actors and the pent-up impulse, nature would lose the human species.
Leonardo da Vinci

PROMISCUITY

Lady Capricorn, he understood, was still keeping open bed.
Aldous Huxley *(1894-1963), English novelist*, Antic Hay, 1923

Eliot: It doesn't suit women to be promiscuous.
Amanda: It doesn't suit men for women to be promiscuous.
Noël Coward *(1899-1973)*, Private Lives

It is as absurd to say that a man can't love one woman all the time as it is to say that a violinist needs several violins to play the same piece of music.
Honoré de Balzac *(1799-1850), French novelist*

The sexual freedom of today for most people is really only a convention, an obligation, a social duty, a social anxiety, a necessary feature of the consumer's way of life.
Pier Paolo Pasolini *(1922-75), Italian film director, writer and poet*

You were born with your legs apart. They'll send you to your grave in a Y-shaped coffin.
Joe Orton *(1933-67), British playwright*

No wearer of a liberty bodice has ever been famed for her promiscuity, and a rarity nowadays of both liberty bodices and virgins is undeniable.
Charlotte Bingham, novelist

She is like measles. Everybody should go through the experience. Once you've had it, you never want to have it again.
A victim of the Grand Duchess Anastasia, who was notorious during the 1930s for entertaining young men

Latins are tenderly enthusiastic. In Brazil they throw flowers at you. In Argentina they throw themselves.
Marlene Dietrich

PROSTITUTION

Prostitution gives her an opportunity to meet people. It provides fresh air and wholesome exercise, and keeps her out of trouble.
Joseph Heller, American novelist, Catch 22, 1961

My method is basically the same as Masters and Johnson, only they charge thousands of dollars and it's called therapy. I charge fifty dollars and it's called prostitution.
Xaviera Hollander American writer and prostitute

Romance without finance is a nuisance. Few men value free merchandise. Let the chippies fall where they may.
Sally Stanford (1904-82), American madam and writer, The Lady of the House, 1966

Fines'd and curl'd hair in the amorous parts, a moist open clint, absence of the membrane hymen, shaggy and discoloured nymphae, the interior orifice of the womb widened, and the voice chang'd is no sufficient evidence of a woman's being a prostitute.
Dr de Venette giving advice to worried husbands in The Mysteries of Conjugal Love Revealed, 1707

There is something utterly nauseating about a system of society which pays a harlot 25 times as much as it pays its Prime Minister, 250 times as much as it pays its Members of Parliament, and 500 times as much as it pays some of its ministers of religion.
Harold Wilson, British politician and former Prime Minister, referring to the case of Christine Keeler, 1963

Prostitutes believe in marriage. It provides them with most of their trade.
'Suzie', quoted in Knave magazine, 1975

It is a silly question to ask a prostitute, why she does it
. . . these are the highest paid of professional women in
America.
Gail Sheehy, Hustling

This is virgin territory for whorehouses.
Al Capone (1899-1947), *Italian-born American gangster, on
suburban Chicago*

We're all hookers. What matters is dignity.
Mike Farren, British writer

Punishing the prostitute promotes the rape of all
women. When prostitution is crime, the message
conveyed is that women who are sexual are 'bad' and
therefore legitimate victims of sexual assault. Sex
becomes a weapon to be used by men.
Margot St James, American activist and prostitute, quoted in the
San Francisco Examiner, 1979

They're whores, and that's not a term of abuse. It's a
good, honest, biblical word for an honourable
profession of ancient lineage. They make love with men
for a living and don't you ever think badly of them for
that. Any woman worthy of the name would do the
same if her children were hungry. Remember, never
judge someone until you've walked a mile in their
moccasins.
Allegra Taylor, Prostitution: 'What's Love Got To Do With It?',
1991

They sit down and drink tea, and the procuress leads in
a Shouma saying, 'pay your respects to the guests' and
the girl does so. Then she commands 'walk forward' –
'turn around' – so the girl turns around to face the light,
and thus to show her face. Then the woman asks, 'let us
see your hands' so the girl pushes up her sleeves to
reveal her hands, arms and her skin. At the command
'look at the guest' she glances sidelong at him, thus
showing her eyes. Then she is asked 'how old are you'
and she gives her reply, so the customer can hear her
voice. The procuress says, 'walk around again', and
pulls back the girl's skirt to reveal her feet.
Chen Dong-Yuan, Chinese writer, describing the ritual of selecting
a young girl for concubinage, Zhongguo Funii Shewnghuo Shi,
1937

I have often noticed that a bribe ... has that effect – it changes a relation. The man who offers a bribe gives away a little of his own importance; the bribe once accepted, he becomes inferior, like a man who has paid for a woman.
Graham Greene *(1904-91), British novelist,* The Comedians, *1966*

If any of your women be guilty of whoredom, then bring your witnesses against them from among themselves, and if they bear witness to the fact, shut them up within their houses till death release them, or God make some way for them.
Koran, seventh century

PUBERTY

All healthy persons, at the time of puberty, must certainly feel the passion of physical love. It is part of their health, and as a natural consequence as hunger or thirst, it is the most delightful of all the passions, and makes the greater part of human happiness.
Dr Michael Ryan, A Manual of Midwifery, *1831*

PUNISHMENT

And if it's true, he should be parted from his bollocks.
*Coal miner **Kenny Mullins**, on NUM President Arthur Scargill, after hearing reports of possible misuse of funds donated during the 1984/85 miners' strike*

Two mothers-in-law.
Lord John Russell (1792-1878) British statesman, on being asked what he would consider a proper punishment for bigamy

RAPE

I strongly feel that a rapist is a rapist, whether he is married to his victim or not.
John Patten, British politician, commenting on the law ruling that a husband can be guilty of raping his wife

RELATIONSHIPS

The easiest kind of relationship for me is with ten
thousand people. The hardest is with one.
Joan Baez, American singer

No, I don't even use the word relationship. Unless
you're screwin' your cousin; that's a 'relationship'.
Anon

RELIGION

I went to a convent in New York and was fired finally
for my insistence that the Immaculate Conception was a
spontaneous combustion.
Dorothy Parker

If I had been the Virgin Mary I would have said no.
Stevie Smith

Personally, I can't see the appeal. Who would put their
faith in a garment whose owner managed to get
pregnant before she even reached for the top button?
*Jaci Stephen, commenting on a piece of cloth allegedly belonging
to the Virgin Mary's nightdress, for sale in Britain*

God is a gentleman. He prefers blondes.
Joe Orton (1933-67), British dramatist, Loot, 1965

Woody Allen was right when someone asked him if he
thought sex was dirty and he said 'if you do it right'.
Sex is not some sort of pristine, reverent ritual. You
want reverence and pristine, go to church.
Cynthia Heimel

Adam and Eve had many advantages but the principal
one was that they escaped teething.
Mark Twain

Whenever Christ was confronted by people in sexual
disarray, he took good care to safeguard sexuality by
reminding them that they had to avoid sin; that is to
say, to use their sexuality in a fully human way.
Dr Jack Dominian

If President Nixon's secretary, Rosemary Woods, had
been Moses secretary, there would only be eight
commandments.
Art Buchwald, 1974

God, why didn't you make women first – when you
were fresh?
Yves Montand *in the film* On a Clear Day You Can See Forever
(screenplay by Alan Jay Lerner)

The good news is that Jesus is coming back. The bad
news is that he's really pissed off.
Bob Hope

R E P U T A T I O N

There are no good girls gone wrong, just bad girls
found out.
Mae West

She: I've heard plenty about your love-making.
He: Oh, it's nothing
She: That's what I heard.
Laugh In, *NBC TV, 1969*

It's the good girls who keep the diaries; the bad girls
never have the time.
Tallulah Bankhead

Funny, really. When you look at the things that go on
these days my story reads like *Noddy.*
Diana Dors

I am as pure as the driven slush.
Tallulah Bankhead

A bad woman always has something she regards as a
curse – a real bit of goodness hidden away somewhere.
Lady Troubridge, *British writer*, The Millionaire, *1907*

My literary reputation – or rather the lack of it – is the
work of male reviewers who fear female sexuality and
don't like successful women.
Erica Jong, *quoted in the* Observer, *1980*

Reluctant though one may be to admit it, the entire
British aristocracy is seamed and honeycombed with
immorality. If you took a pin and jabbed it down
anywhere in the pages of *Debrett's Peerage* you would
find it piercing the name of someone with a conscience
as tender as a sunburned neck.
P. G. Wodehouse, *Mulliner Nights, 1933*

When the Himalayan peasant meets the he-bear in his pride, he shouts to scare the monster, who will often turn aside. But the she-bear thus accosted rends the peasant tooth and nail. For the female of the species is more deadly than the male.
Rudyard Kipling (1865-1936), Indian-born British writer, The Female of the Species

Sade brushes the lust off the labia of women asphyxiated in the smoky cell of sex.
Som Deva, Indian sexologist, describing the activities of the Marquis de Sade, The Marching Eros, 1983

The worst lay in the world. She was always drunk and she was always eating.
Peter Lawford, actor, on Rita Hayworth

I used to be snow white but I drifted.
Mae West

ROMANCE

Give me my golf clubs, fresh air and a beautiful partner, and you can keep my golf clubs and the fresh air.
Jack Benny

There is never any real sex in romance; what is more, there is very little, and that of a very crude kind, in ninety-nine hundredths of our married life.
George Bernard Shaw

Oh, what a dear, ravishing thing is the beginning of an amour!
Aphra Behn (1640-89), English novelist and playwright

I know a lot of people didn't expect our relationship to last – but we've just celebrated our two months anniversary.
Britt Ekland, speaking of her latest partner

To love oneself is the beginning of a life-long romance.
Oscar Wilde

She was a lovely girl. Our courtship was fast and furious – I was fast and she was furious.
Max Kauffmann

A silvery June afternoon. A June afternoon in Paris 23 years ago. And I am standing in the courtyard of the Palais Royal scanning its tall windows and wondering which of them belong to the apartment of Colette, the Grande Mademoiselle of French letters.
Truman Capote, quoted in the Daily Telegraph *magazine*

How can I be a maid and sleep every night with the King? When he comes to bed he kisses me, takes me by the hand and bids me 'Goodnight, Sweetheart,' and in the morning, he kisses me and bids me 'Farewell darling!' Is not this enough?
Anne of Cleves (1515-57), fourth wife of King Henry VIII, on being asked by her lady-in-waiting if she was still a maid

I don't know what the word means. It sounds as if it's something to do with knights in shining armour.
Daphne du Maurier (1907-89), British novelist and playwright, on romance

If there is to be any romance in marriage women must be given every chance to earn a decent living at other occupations. Otherwise no man can be sure that he is loved for himself alone, and that his wife did not come to the registry office because she had no luck at the labour exchange.
Rebecca West (1892-1983), British novelist, The Art of Being Ruled, *1920*

The word 'romantic' doesn't exist in the male vocabulary in Leeds. A date means a walk round the pub and a packet of crisps if he's in a generous mood. If you're really lucky, he'll buy you a take-away.
A secretary from Leeds quoted in the Daily Mirror

As romantic as the sound of hogs being butchered.
Truman Capote describing James Thurber and girlfriend making love

I am a romantic. Love affairs are the only real education in life.
Marlene Dietrich

SEDUCTION

The resistance of a woman is not always proof of her virtue, but more often of her experience.
Ninon de Lenclos

A woman will sometimes forgive the man who tries to seduce her, but never the man who misses an opportunity when offered.
Charles-Maurice de Talleyrand (1754-1838), French bishop and politician

The trouble with Ian is that he gets off with more women because he can't get on with them.
Rosamund Lehmann, British author, on Ian Fleming

Men who do not make advances to women are apt to become victims of women who make advances to them.
Walter Bagehot

To succeed with the opposite sex, tell her you're impotent. She can't wait to disprove it.
Cary Grant (1904-86), actor

He in a few minutes ravished this fair creature, or at least would have ravished her, if she had not, by a timely compliance, prevented him.
Henry Fielding

When Venus said, 'spell No for me',
'N-O' Dan Cupid wrote with glee,
and smiled at his success:
'Ah, child,' said Venus, laughing low,
'We women do not spell it so,
we spell it Y-E-S.'
Carolyn Wells (1869-1942), American writer and humorist, The Spelling Lesson, 1920

What they [girls] love to yield they would often rather have stolen. Rough seduction delights them, the boldness of near rape is a compliment.
Ovid (43BC-AD17), The Art of Love

I tried to charm the pants off Bob Dylan but everyone will be disappointed to learn that I was unsuccessful. I got close . . . a couple of fast feels in the front seat of his Cadillac.
Bette Midler, American actress and singer, quoted in Rolling Stone magazine, 1982

Shopping can be fun. It can be an emotional outlet. Women go shopping to buy friendship and flattery from the assistant. For some women, shopping is a sex compensation, so the shop must seduce the customer.
Lady Dartmouth, British politician and hostess

I distinguish between terror and fear. From terror one escapes screaming, but fear has an odd seduction. Fear and the sense of sex are linked in secret conspiracy, but terror is a sickness like hate.
Graham Greene, Ways of Escape, *1980*

SELF-CONTROL

My own reaction to these men with this powerful sex appeal is secretly and passionately responsive – but shamefully, and secretly. So, I long to acquiesce, to fling my flesh at their feet. To have them hurt and humiliate me, however they may wish. My instinctive urge is to accept the role of victim to their villainy – I would do anything to engage their attention . . . but instead, alas, I practise control.
Molly Parkin, *British writer and columnist*, Good Golly Miss Molly

SELF-KNOWLEDGE

Ah! Madam . . . you know everything in the world but your perfections, and you only know not those, because 'tis the top of perfection not to know them.
William Congreve *(1670-1729), English dramatist*

Shame is the feeling you have when you agree with the woman who loves you that you are the man she thinks you are.
Carl Sandburg *(1878-1967), American poet*

I found that I became more sexually confident, that I could even have entertained the likes of empty-headed beach boys in my bed, if I'd found their bodies desirable enough.
Molly Parkin *on her new-found confidence after divorce*

Sexual freedom has become more important than identity. Indeed, it has superseded it. The modern philosophy states – I ejaculate, therefore I am.
Quentin Crisp, *British writer*, How to Become a Virgin, *1981*

SENSES

The intoxication of rouge is an insidious vintage known to more girls than mere man can ever believe.
Dorothy Speare (1898-1951), American writer, Dancers in the Dark, 1922

SEX

Older women are best because they always think they may be doing it for the last time.
Ian Fleming

Whoever named it necking was a poor judge of anatomy.
Groucho Marx

The only reason I would take up jogging is so I could hear heavy breathing again.
Erma Bombeck

Sex is not only a divine and beautiful activity: it's a murderous activity. People kill each other in bed. Some of the greatest crimes ever committed were committed in bed. And no weapons were used.
Norman Mailer, American writer

I know nothing about sex, because I was always married.
Zsa Zsa Gabor

When I'm good I'm very good, but when I'm bad I'm better.
Mae West

My own belief is that there is hardly anyone whose sexual life, if it were broadcast, would not fill the world at large with surprise and horror.
W. Somerset Maugham

Maybe I'm not talented. Maybe I'm just the Dinah Shore of the sixties. The square people think I'm too hip and the hip people think I'm too square. And nobody likes my choice of men – everybody thinks I'm fucking the Mormon Tabernacle Choir.
Cher

It's like sex. You can't describe it until you've
experienced it.
Stanley Kalms, *founder and chairman of the Dixons Group plc,*
talking about High Definition Television

I don't see much of Alfred any more since he got so
interested in sex.
Mrs Alfred Kinsey, *wife of the author of the Kinsey Report on*
sexual behaviour

The tragedy is when you've got sex in the head instead
of down where it belongs.
D. H. Lawrence

Love is the answer, but while you're waiting for the
answer, sex raises some pretty good questions.
Woody Allen

You remember your first mountain in much the same
way you remember having your first sexual experience,
except that climbing doesn't make as much mess and
you don't cry for a week if Ben Nevis forgets to phone
next morning.
Muriel Gray, *TV presenter and writer,* The First Fifty, *1990*

I think I made his back feel better.
Marilyn Monroe, *after a private meeting with John F. Kennedy*

I get very sexually excited on stage. It's like making love
to 9,000 people at once.
Prince

I'd rather have a nice cup of tea.
Boy George

Is sex dirty? Only if its done right.
Woody Allen

There are a lot more interesting things in life than sex –
like reading.
Jean Alexander, *the actress who played Hilda Ogden in ITV's*
Coronation Street

Boats, cars, sex . . . you have to touch all of them lightly
or they lose their glamour.
Mel Gibson, *Australian actor*

It's the most fun I ever had without laughing.
Woody Allen

Most of the time, women want it more than men. I do.
Donna Ewin, page three girl

Sex is good for you. I'd rather die making love than in any other way.
Edward Woodward, British actor

People have always found my sex life of interest, but I can do without sex.
Pamella Bordes, call-girl turned photographer

They say sex is as good as a five-mile run. I don't think I move five miles making love, but we've got three bedrooms. Make of that what you will.
Michael Palin, British actor and writer

Good sex is absolutely wonderful for you – much better than jogging.
Jilly Cooper

When two people make love, there are at least four people present – the two who are actually there and the two they are thinking about.
Sigmund Freud

Sex in a love relationship is always better. I know a lot more about sex now – there's no more of that frantic fumbling and groping that went on when you were young.
Paul Daniels, magician

Lady Rumpers: And then you took me.
Sir Percy: I took *you*? You took *me*. Your land army breeches came down with a fluency born of long practice.
Alan Bennett, Habeus Corpus, 1973

I wish I had as much in bed as I get in the newspapers.
Linda Ronstadt

I'd like to do a love scene with him just to see what all the yelling is about.
Shirley Maclaine on her brother Warren Beatty

There will be sex after death – we just won't be able to feel it.
Lily Tomlin

I believe in sex and death – two experiences that come once in a lifetime.
Woody Allen, The Sleeper, 1973

I know it does make people happy but to me it is just like having a cup of tea.
Cynthia Payne *after her acquittal over the famous sex-for-luncheon-vouchers case, 1987*

It was just one of those things which, if you had been to bed before marriage, you would presumably have known.
Barbara Cartland

Watch sex. It is the key to success and the trap-door to failure.
Michael Shea, *Director of Public Affairs, Hanson plc*

Last time I tried to make love to my wife nothing was happening, so I said to her, what's the matter, you can't think of anybody either?
Rodney Dangerfield

I would rather go to bed with Lillian Russell stark naked than Ulysses Grant in full military regalia.
Mark Twain

If it weren't for pickpockets I'd have no sex life at all.
Rodney Dangerfield

Sex is nobody's business except for the five people involved.
Anon

Sex is the biggest nothing of all time.
Andy Warhol

All this fuss about sleeping together. For physical pleasure I'd sooner go to my dentist any day.
Evelyn Waugh

Nothing is so much to be shunned as sex relations.
St Augustine *(354-430)*

Are you going to come quietly or do I have to use earplugs?
The Goon Show

The physical union of the sexes ... only intensifies
man's sense of solitude.
Nikolai Berdyaev (1874-1948), Russian philosopher

They made love as though they were an endangered
species.
Peter de Vries

In sexual intercourse it's quality not quantity that
counts.
Dr David Reuben

Make love to every woman you meet. If you get five per
cent on your outlays, it's a good investment.
Arnold Bennett

Of the delights of this world man cares most for sexual
intercourse, yet he has left it out of his heaven.
Mark Twain

Whatever else can be said about sex, it cannot be called
a dignified performance.
Helen Lawrenson

Women complain about sex more than men. Their
gripes fall into two major categories: (1) Not enough;
(2) Too much.
Ann Landers

In fact, it's quite ridiculous, the shapes people throw
when they get down to it. There are few positions more
ridiculous to look at than the positions people adopt
when they are together. Limbs everywhere. Orifices
gaping. Mucus pouring out and in. Sweat flying. Sheets
wrecked. Animals and insects fleeing the scene when the
going gets rough. Noise? My dear, the evacuation of
Dunkirk in World War Two was an intellectual
discussion compared to it. Once in a while, of course,
there's silence. Usually afterwards. It's called
exhaustion.
Nell McCafferty

I like a man what takes his time.
Mae West

It is depressing to have to insist that sex is not an
unnecessary, morally dubious self-indulgence but a
basic human need, no less for women than for men.
Ellen Willis

Basically, heterosexuality means men first. That's what it's all about.
Charlotte Bunch

Ducking for apples – change one letter and it's the story of my life.
Dorothy Parker

Some men are all right in their place – if they only knew the right places.
Mae West

In real life women are always trying to mix something up with sex – religion, or babies, or hard cash; it is only men who long for sex separated out, without rings or strings.
Katherine Whitehorn

I'd rather have a good bowl of soup.
Margaret Houston

All too many men still seem to believe, in a rather naïve and egocentric way, that what feels good to them is automatically what feels good to women.
Shere Hite, American researcher and writer

I've tried several varieties of sex. The conventional position makes me claustrophobic. And the others either give me a stiff neck or lockjaw.
Tallulah Bankhead

The truth is that sex doesn't mean that much to me now.
Lana Turner, American actress

I am happy now that Charles calls on my bed chamber less frequently than of old. As it is, I now endure but two calls a week and when I hear his steps outside my door I lie down on my bed, close my eyes, open my legs and think of England.
Lady Alice Hillingdon, 1912

Oh, not at all – just a straight-away pounder
Lily Langtry, on being asked if the Prince of Wales was a romantic lover

My husband is German; every night I get dressed up like Poland and he invades me.
Bette Midler

As for the topsy turvy tangle known as *soixante-neuf*, personally I have always felt it to be madly confusing, like trying to pat your head and rub your stomach at the same time.
Helen Lawrenson

Conventional sexual intercourse is like squirting jam into a doughnut.
Germaine Greer

When grown-ups do it it's kind of dirty – that's because there's no one to punish them.
Tuesday Weld, American actress

The important thing in acting is to be able to laugh and cry. If I have to cry, I think of my sex life. If I have to laugh, I think of my sex life.
Glenda Jackson

I didn't know how babies were made until I was pregnant with my fourth child five years later.
Loretta Lynn

I didn't get ahead by sleeping with people. Girls take heart.
Barbara Walters

I have never been able to sleep with anyone. I require a full-size bed so that I can lie in the middle of it and extend my arms spreadeagle on both sides without being obstructed.
Mae West

I've only slept with the men I've been married to. How many women can make that claim?
Elizabeth Taylor

Personally, I like sex and I don't care what a man thinks of me as long as I get what I want from him – which is usually sex.
Valerie Perrine, American actress

I've never taken up with a congressman in my life . . . I've never gone below the Senate.
Barbara Howar

Ignorance of the necessity for sexual intercourse to the health and virtue of both man and woman, is the most fundamental error in medical and moral philosophy.
George Drysdale, The Elements of Social Science, *1854*

So many Englishwomen look upon sexual intercourse as abhorrent and not as a natural fulfilment of true love. My wife considered all bodily desire to be nothing less than animal passion, and that true love between husband and wife should be purely mental and not physical . . . like so many Englishwomen she considered that any show of affection was not in keeping with her dignity as a woman and that all lovemaking and caresses should come entirely from the man and that the woman should be the passive receiver of affection.
Anonymous letter to Marie Stopes, 1921

I have long lost any capacity for surprise where sex is concerned.
Geoffrey Howard (1889-1973), British judge

But did thee feel the earth move?
Ernest Hemingway, For Whom the Bell Tolls, 1940

No sex without responsibility.
Lord Longford, British politician and social reformer

'Sex,' she says, 'is a subject like any other subject. Every bit as interesting as agriculture.'
Muriel Spark, The Hothouse by the East River, 1973

The reproduction of mankind is a great marvel and mystery. Had God consulted me in the matter, I should have advised him to continue the generation of the species by fashioning them of clay.
Martin Luther

This sex attraction, though it is useful for keeping the world peopled, has nothing to do with beauty: it blinds us to ugliness instead of opening our eyes to beauty.
George Bernard Shaw

It has to be admitted that we English have sex on the brain, which is a very unsatisfactory place to have it.
Malcolm Muggeridge, British journalist

Sex is. There is nothing more to be done about it. Sex builds no roads, writes no novels and sex certainly gives no meaning to anything in life but itself.
Gore Vidal

Sex is a pleasurable exercise in plumbing, but be careful or you'll get yeast in your drain pipe.
Rita Mae Brown

Two young lovers left rescuers all at sea when they were caught making love in a rubber dinghy. People on shore at Saltdean, near Brighton, saw the little craft moving violently and thought two children were stranded. But rescuers were sent packing after the lovers told them they could cope on their own. A spokesman said, 'They saved some energy for the row home.'
Newspaper report, April 1992

And remember, there's nothing these women won't do to satisfy their ever-moist groins; they've just one obsession – sex.
Juvenal (c.AD60-140), Roman satirist and poet, Satires X

I enjoy fucking my wife. She lets me do it any way I want. No women's liberation for her. Lots of male chauvinist pig.
Joseph Heller, American novelist, Something Happened, 1974

No one, thank goodness, advocates that people should go about with long green strands of snot dangling from their noses in the name of nasal freedom, yet quite a few people have been converted in recent years to a belief that it is permissible for them to inflict the sights, sounds and smells of their bodies on any innocent bystander in the name of 'sexual freedom'.
Quentin Crisp

The man and woman make love, attain climax, fall separate. Then she whispers, 'I'll tell you who I was thinking of if you tell me who you were thinking of.' Like most sex jokes the origins of the pleasant exchange are obscure. But whatever the source, it seldom fails to evoke a certain awful recognition.
Gore Vidal

The zipless fuck is absolutely pure . . . and is rarer than the unicorn.
Erica Jong, Fear of Flying

Sex is one of the nine reasons for reincarnation. The other eight are unimportant.
Henry Miller, Big Sur and the Oranges of Hieronymus Bosch, 1957

Sex – the poor man's polo.
Clifford Odets (attrib)

In the case of very fascinating women, sex is a
challenge, not a defence.
Oscar Wilde, An Ideal Husband

Sex is like having dinner – sometimes you joke about
the dishes, sometimes you take the meal seriously.
Woody Allen

Sex ought to be a wholly satisfying link between two
affectionate people from which they emerge unanxious,
rewarded and ready for more.
Dr Alex Comfort, British sexologist, The Joy of Sex, 1972

Have you not as yet observed that pleasure, which is
undeniably the sole motive force behind the union of
the sexes, is nevertheless not enough to form a bond
between them? And that, if it is preceded by desire
which impels, it is succeeded by disgust which repels?
That is a law of nature which love alone can alter.
Pierre Choderlos de Laclos (1741-1803), French novelist, Les
Liaisons Dangereuses, 1782

The total deprivation of sex produces irritability.
Elizabeth Blackwell (1821-1910), American physician, The
Human Element in Sex

It's all this cold-hearted fucking that is death and idiocy.
D. H. Lawrence, Lady Chatterley's Lover, 1928

A well-bred woman does not seek carnal gratification,
and she is usually apathetic to sexual pleasures. Her
love is physical or spiritual rather than carnal, and her
passiveness in regard to coition often amounts to
disgust for it. Lust is seldom an element in a women's
character, and she is the preserver of chastity and
morality.
Dr O. A. Wall, Sex and Sex Worship, 1932

To know women as well as I do: they are only unwilling
when you compel them, but after they're as enthusiastic
as you are.
Jean Giraudoux (1882-1944), French dramatist, Tiger at the
Gates, 1935

Sex is exciting only when it is a subtle and pervasive
part of the relationship between men and women,
varying in its form from adolescence to old age, and it
dies only with death if is properly nourished in life.
Pearl Buck (1892-1973), Nobel prize-winning American novelist

The Kama Sutra is the Mrs Beeton of sex.
Aldous Huxley, quoted in the Sunday Times, *1973*

Sex is interesting, but it's not totally important. I mean it's not even as important (physically) as excretion. A man can go seventy years without a piece of ass, but he can die in a week without a bowel movement.
Charles Bukowski, American writer, Notes on a Dirty Old Man

Sexual intercourse is kicking death in the ass while singing.
Charles Bukowski

When a man and a woman of unorthodox tastes make love the man could be said to be introducing his foible into her quirk.
Kenneth Tynan, the Guardian, *1975*

It is better to be first with an ugly woman than the hundredth with a beauty.
Pearl Buck, The Good Earth

SEX AIDS

There are a number of mechanical devices which increase sexual arousal, particularly in women. Chief among these is the Mercedes-Benz 380SL convertible.
P. J. O'Rourke

Sometimes a cigar is just a cigar.
Sigmund Freud, on being asked by a student whether his cigar-smoking was a symbolic activity

Maybe I'll make a 'Mary Poppins' movie and shove the umbrella up my ass.
Marilyn Chambers

Det-Inspector Roy Penrose said in a statement read to the court that a booklet advertising artificial male organs was found by police at Miss Jones's home in May. They also found a vibrating device hidden inside a pouffe. The hearing continues today.
Report in the Birmingham Post, *quoted in* Private Eye *magazine*

Our first declared confrontation was over sex. As part of my new-broom policy at Mount Street, I systematically invaded cupboards and drawers throwing out old make-up bottles, other women's clothes, and objects that could only have been there for sexual use: a cork on a long string attached to a hot-water bottle, a pair of Victorian knickers, and a single black stocking.
Kathleen Tynan on married life with Kenneth Tynan

Woman caller: I was really disgusted when I opened the parcel all these dangly bits fell out, I was so embarrassed.
Radio presenter: Did you not realise you had sent off for a sex aid?
Caller: No, I bought it to surprise my daughter. A few years ago I bought her an inflatable deer to sit in her garden. It looked good, very realistic – until the kids punctured it. So, I thought I'd buy her the sheep to replace it!
Conversation on LBC Radio talk show, March 1992, regarding a product marketed under the title of 'Love Ewe'

SEX APPEAL

If a man doesn't look at me when I walk into a room, he's gay.
Kathleen Turner, American actress

Nothing risqué, nothing gained.
Alexander Woollcott

We need heroes. Whether or not it pleases you, Mr Connery, we have decided that you will be our hero.
Princess Anne at a film première

I thought I couldn't afford to take her out and smoke as well. So I gave up cigarettes. Then I took her out and one day I looked at her and thought: 'Oh well', and I went back to smoking again, and that was better.
Benny Hill, on a girlfriend he had when earning 27s 6d a week

These are very confusing times. For the first time in history a woman is expected to combine intelligence with a sharp hairdo, a raised consciousness with high heels, and an open, non-sexist relationship with a tan guy who has a great bod.
Lynda Barry, Why are Women Crazy? *cartoon in* Esquire *magazine, 1984*

Good rock stars take drugs, put their penises in plaster of Paris, collectivise their sex, molest policemen, promote self-curiosity, unlock myriad spirits, epitomise fun, freedom and bullshit. Can the business anarchist on your block match that?
Richard Neville, Australian journalist, Playpower, *1970*

I can't speak for women, but I find Mikhail Gorbachev attractive as a man's man. It's an extraordinary combination of intelligence, baldness and serenity.
Sean Connery

I'm more the thinking woman's crumbling ruin. I always wear the same suit on the programme so people don't notice me.
Melvyn Bragg, host of the South Bank Show, *on the suggestion that he was 'the thinking woman's crumpet'*

I have had propositions, but I don't take them up. The family can't understand how anyone can fancy me. But then, neither can I.
Barry Norman, film critic

Many a man in love with a dimple makes the mistake of marrying the wrong girl.
Stephen Leacock, English-born Canadian economist and humorist, Literary Lapses, *1910*

I'm in my seventies. What could she possibly see in me – is she into necrophilia or something?
Dirk Bogarde, British actor and novelist, on a request by Madonna to include him in her book Sex

Glenda Jackson, when she stepped up to accept her
Oscar wrapped in an old horse-blanket and with her
curlers almost hidden under a used tea towel, she yet
generated more real sexuality than any of the so-called
'glamour' stars in the Hollywood Bowl. A corrosively
intelligent actress. The thinking man's Hilda Ogden.
Henry Root, *quoted in* World of Knowledge

Scotsmen are metaphysical and emotional, they are
sceptical and mystical, they are romantic and ironic,
they are cruel and tender, and full of mirth and despair.
Rachel Annand Taylor, William Dunbar, *1931*

Plunging necklines attract more attention and cost less
money.
Shelley Winters, *American actress, quoted in the* Sunday Times,
1971

She sounded like the Book of Revelations read out over
a railway station public-address system by a
headmistress of a certain age, wearing calico knickers.
Clive James *describing Margaret Thatcher on television*

All a writer has to do to get a woman is to say he's a
writer. It's an aphrodisiac.
Saul Bellow, *American novelist*

If Canada is underdeveloped, so is Brigitte Bardot.
H. R. Macmillan

Brigitte Bardot on the screen is not simply a selfish
delinquent. She has freshness, charm and a touch of
mischievousness. She is irresponsible and immoral, but
not deliberately cruel.
The Observer, *1959*

He who hath a long and great nose is an admirer of the
fair sex, and well accomplished for the war of Venus.
Aristotle

SEX EDUCATION

Edinburgh's Director of Education, referring to sex
education, is reported to have said: 'Teachers noticed a
new look in children's eyes after an experimental
course.'
Reported in the Sunday Express

Few of them wished to proceed to further education.
The girls were dreaming of boys and babies, and the
boys of sheep and whisky.
Reported in the Glasgow Evening Times

All teaching in all subjects aims to stimulate interest. It
would be odd if this were not true of sex lessons.
Roger Probert, Birmingham headmaster, 1973

SEXUAL DREAM / FANTASY

. . . Deaf and dumb (except when I ask her to talk
dirty); her father owns a wine store; gives me no crap
about anything on earth, gives me all over body
massages, and doesn't say things like 'have you come,
can I get dressed now?'
Anon

Dear Sir,
I hope I am not a prude, but I feel compelled to lodge a
protest concerning the ever increasing flood of obscenity
in dreams. Many of my friends have been shocked and
sickened as myself by the filth that is poured out nightly
as soon as our eyes are closed. It is certainly not my idea
of home entertainment. Night after night, the most
disgraceful scenes of perversion and bestiality are
perpetuated behind my eyelids . . . it is imperative that
official action should be taken.
Kenneth Tynan, The Sound of Two Hands Clapping, 1978

Of course, as a teenager my sexual fantasies were full of
Anita Ekberg and the usual giant Nordic goddesses.
That is until Brigitte Bardot became the 'love of my life'
in the late fifties. All my girlfriends who were dark-
haired suffered under my constant pressure to become
Brigitte. By the time I married my first wife (who was, I
think, a natural auburn), she too had become a long-
haired blonde with the obligatory bangs.
    I met the real Brigitte a few years later. I was on acid
and she was on the way out.
John Lennon

SEXIST

If I really felt I was being sexist in my shows, I'd stop.
As it is, my fan mail from women carries every kind of
postmark from around the world – and every kind of
suggestion.
Benny Hill

SEX ON THE AIR

Millions buy certain newspapers so they can read about
sex and boobs. I give it to them over the air.
Tony Blackburn, *radio presenter and disc-jockey*

Only yesterday a cab driver told me he had driven into
the back of a car when I asked a woman to twang her
suspenders. I love stockings and suspenders. I even wear
them myself to prove I'm not sexist. It's a turn-on.
Tony Blackburn, *claiming that the secret of his success on Radio
London was the free and frank way sex was discussed on his
programme. A few months after his claim, Radio London was
disbanded.*

SEX AND FILMS

There are a lot of chicks who get laid by the director
and still don't get the part.
Claudia Linnear, *American singer*

A movie without sex would be like a candy bar without
nuts.
Earl Wilson, *American columnist*

Do not think that the solution to man's solitude is a line
of men masturbating and a line of women
masturbating.
Lina Wertmuller, *Italian film director*

Sex is emotion in motion.
Mae West

Even if the whole thing, including what she did on the
screen, has evolved from the sort of girl she was, her life
and career still seem to have been dreamed up by one of
her scriptwriters.
David Shipman, *British publisher, on the actress Clara Bow*

SEX AND ROCK AND ROLL

A game is a closed field, a ring of death with, oh, sex as the centre. Performing is the only game I've got.
Jim Morrison (1943-71), lead singer of The Doors

Pop music is sex and you have to hit them in the face with it.
Andrew Loog Oldham, British rock manager

The wriggling ponces of the spoken word.
D. G. Bridson on disc jockeys

Purgative of all frustrations. It's like going to Confession when I was ten years old. The weight of wanking would lift from my brain as I told the priest I'd masturbated X times. At gigs it's the same thing.
Bob Geldof, Irish singer

Rock and roll is about cocks and jiving and the odd bloody nose . . . and about people like us talking seriously about the social order.
Jean-Jacques Burnel, guitarist with The Stranglers, quoted in the New Musical Express, *1979*

You're all a bunch of fucking idiots. Your faces are being pressed into the shit of the world. Take your fucking friend and love him. Do you want to see my cock?
Jim Morrison, taking a direct approach with female fans

SEX AND VERBOSITY

For three days they went at it without repose, showing the way the millrace flows, and how the industrious spindle goes. They gave the lamb suck, they startled the buck, they tried on the finger ring for luck. They cradled the child, they kissed the twins, they polished the sword till it had not a speck, they taught the sparrow how to peck, they made the camel show his neck, and fed the bird at the barley bins. They gave the little pigeon seed, and put the rabbit out to feed, with many another pretty deed, till they blew a hole in the shepherd's reed.
Pastrycook's Tale, The Arabian Nights

SEX SYMBOL

A sex symbol becomes a thing. I hate being a thing.
Marilyn Monroe (1926-62)

Can't act . . . voice like a tight squeak . . . utterly unsure
of herself . . . unable even to take refuge in her own
insignificance.
Columbia Pictures comments on Marilyn Monroe

A vacuum with nipples.
Otto Preminger, American film director, on Marilyn Monroe

She was good at playing abstract confusion in the same
way that a midget is good at being short.
Clive James on Marilyn Monroe

Marilyn was mean. Terribly mean. The meanest woman
I ever met around this town. I have never met anybody
as mean as Marilyn Monroe or as utterly fabulous on
the screen, and that includes Garbo.
Billy Wilder, American writer and film director

To put it bluntly, I seem to be a whole superstructure
with no foundation. But I'm working on the
foundation.
Marilyn Monroe

What's so fucking wrong with being a sex symbol?
Kris Kristofferson, American singer and actor

Being a sex symbol is a heavy load to carry, especially
when one is tired, hurt and bewildered.
Clara Bow (1905-65), American actress

SEXUALITY

Sexuality is something like nuclear energy, which may
prove amenable to domestication, through scruple, but
then again may not.
Susan Sontag, American essayist, Styles of Radical Will, 1969

No man can be held throughout the day by what
happens throughout the night.
*Sally Stanford, American madame and writer, The Lady of the
House, 1966*

Her body is arranged the way it is to display it to the man looking at the picture. The picture is made to appeal to his sexuality. It has nothing to do with her sexuality . . . women are there to feed an appetite, not to have any of their own.

John Berger, British writer and critic, on the construction of advertising images, Ways of Seeing, 1972

S E X Y

Madame Bovary is the sexiest book imaginable. The woman's virtually a nymphomaniac but you won't find a vulgar word in the entire thing.
Noël Coward

Being bald is an unfailing sex magnet.
Telly Savalas, actor

It's a flesh market, you won't find finer flesh anywhere.
Julia Morley, British organiser of Miss World

Shakespeare is the sexiest great writer in the language.
A. L. Rowse, British academic

. . . as a vandalised launderama.
Victoria Wood, comedienne

. . . as a side of bacon in the deep freeze.
Les Dawson, comedian

. . . as a man making love with his socks on.
Anon

Well built without being the slightest bit sexy, like a junior minister's wife.
Denis Norden

Perhaps it was time to stretch a bit. The truth is, I didn't want to do those glamorous leading-men roles for ever. I'm much better at playing villains, or slightly villainous guys. It's more fun and it's definitely more sexy.
Michael Douglas

I've spent time with her and she's everything a man could want. She's a very warm, beautiful, intelligent and sexy lady.
Sylvester Stallone on Sarah Ferguson, the Duchess of York

George Moore unexpectedly pinched my behind. I felt rather honoured that my behind should have drawn the attention of the great master of English prose.
Ilka Chase, American actress and author

You don't have to hit anybody on the head with four-letter words to be sexy.
Eartha Kitt, singer

I am the world's sexiest man.
Noël Coward

SINS

Nothing makes one so vain as being told that one is a sinner.
Oscar Wilde

Few love to hear the sins they love to act.
William Shakespeare, Pericles

SUCCESS

A lot of executives keep up the pretence of being solid community members when they are sleeping with their secretaries. Hef's honest. He isn't burdened by success.
Christie Hefner, Chief Executive of Playboy Enterprises, on her father

Anyone can have a key to the executive washroom, but once a woman gets inside, what is there? A lavatory.
Germaine Greer

The secret is to marry an older woman.
Peter Tickner, about to celebrate 74 years of marriage – both he and his wife Rose are 100

For a penniless, pregnant, Brazilian girl, Ron's a prime catch.
Charmain Brent, on hearing that her train-robber husband, Ronald Biggs, had found another woman

Beardsley is now on top and working hard to get it.
Jim Rosenthal, commentator, on Peter Beardsley's soccer technique

My biggest problem all my life was men. I never met
one yet who could compete with the image the public
made out of Bette Davis.
Bette Davis *(1908-89), American actress,* Conversations in the
Raw

If I wrote a play about my own life people would be far
more shocked. I feel sex is a good thing. It makes people
better people, and I think that desiring and loving, and
even having people, is the best thing life has to offer.
Nell Dunn, *playwright and novelist, commenting on her play* Up
the Junction

You have to admit that most women who have done
something with their lives have been disliked by almost
everyone.
Françoise Gilot, painter and mistress of Picasso, 1987

TALL STORIES

Girl: I saw you the other day at the corner of
Hollywood and Vine winking at the girls.
Rudy Vallee: I wasn't winking, that's a windy corner.
Something got in my eye.
Girl: She got in your car too.
The Rudy Vallee Show, c.*1920*

We were rehearsing a love scene and Whitney needed help.
Kevin Costner, *when caught kissing Whitney Houston behind a trailer on film set*

It was so romantic. He just took it out and put it on the table in Soho.
Kathryn Holloway, *presenter of TV AM, showing off her engagement ring to the TV-AM presenters and viewers*

The more undeveloped the country the more overdeveloped the women.
J. K. Galbraith, Time, 1969

No woman came amiss to him if they were very willing and very fat. The standard of His Majesty's taste made all those ladies who aspired to his favour and who were near the statutable size strain and swell themselves like frogs in the fable to rival the bulk and dignity of the ox. Some succeeded and others burst.
Lord Chesterfield, *writing about King George I*

TEMPTATION

The only way to get rid of temptation is to yield to it . . .
I can resist everything but temptation.
Oscar Wilde

What makes resisting temptation difficult for many people is they don't want to discourage it completely.
Franklin P. Jones

I am not over-fond of resisting temptation.
William Beckford (1759-1844), *English author*

Do you really think it is weakness that yields to temptation? I tell you that there are terrible temptations which it requires strength, strength and courage to yield to.
Oscar Wilde

Why resist temptation – there will always be more.
Don Herold, *American humorist, writer and artist*

A little of what you fancy does you good.
Marie Lloyd (1870-1922), *British music-hall entertainer*

Ah, why did God,
creator wise that peopled highest heaven
with spirits masculine, create at last
this novelty on earth, this fair defect
of nature, woman?
John Milton (1608-74), *English poet*, Paradise Lost, 1667

The right education of the female sex, as it is in a
manner everywhere neglected, so it ought to be
generally lamented. Most in this depraved later age
think a woman learned and wise enough if she can
distinguish her husband's bed from another's.
Mrs Hannah Woolley (1623-75), *English governess*, The
Gentlewoman's Companion, 1675

THERAPY

They all sit around feeling very spiritual, with their
mental hands on each other's knees, discussing sex as if
it were the art of Fugue.
John Osborne, *British playwright*, Look Back in Anger

TIME

Is there a cure for a broken heart? Only time can heal
your broken heart, just as time can heal his broken
arms and legs.
Miss Piggy, Miss Piggy's Guide to Life, 1981

TRADITION

I was raised in the Jewish tradition, taught never to
marry a gentile woman, shave on a Saturday and, more
especially never to shave a gentile woman on Saturday.
Woody Allen

TRUE CONFESSIONS

When I have one foot in the grave I will tell the truth
about women. I shall tell it, jump into my coffin, pull
the lid over me and say, 'Do what you like now.'
Tolstoy

I don't care what is written about me so long as it isn't true.
Dorothy Parker

A good source of humour is the relationship between the sexes. And it is always the man who comes off worst in what I do – never the woman. Terrible things happen to me and the other men in my shows. Teeth come out; we get knocked on the head hard. But the girls retain their dignity: it is the men who are the idiots. And that is true in real life as well.
Benny Hill

A woman reading *Playboy* feels a little like a Jew reading a Nazi manual.
Gloria Steinem

I never know how much of what I say is true.
Bette Midler

At certain times I like sex – like after a cigarette.
Rodney Dangerfield

Look, Mr President, I might sleep with them, but I'm damned if I'll eat lunch with them.
Bill Lawrence, American politician, to John F. Kennedy, on the subject of admitting women to the all-male Gridiron Club

It's all right letting yourself go, as long as you can get yourself back.
Mick Jagger, British rock star

I like making love myself and I can make love for about three minutes. Three minutes of serious fucking and I need eight hours sleep and a bowl of wheaties.
Richard Pryor, American comedian and actor, Richard Pryor in Concert, 1980

VAGINA

The vagina walls are quite insensitive in the great majority of females . . . there is no evidence that the vagina is ever the sole source of arousal, or even the primary source of erotic arousal in any female.
Alfred Charles Kinsey (1894-1956), American zoologist and director of the Institute for Sex Research, Sexual Behaviour in the Human Female, 1953

In the third stage they get their pleasure chiefly from the
little penis that they have on the outside of their bodies,
called the clitoris, and are mostly interested in having
that organ stimulated. In the adult stage they get their
greatest pleasure from the vagina, which can be used
much more effectively to give pleasure to a male
partner.
Eric Berne, British doctor, A Layman's Guide to Psychiatry and
Psychoanalysis, *1969*

V I C E S

One reason I don't drink is that I want to know when
I'm having a good time.
Nancy, Lady Astor

Cocaine isn't habit-forming. I should know – I've been
using it for years.
Tallulah Bankhead

It seems impossible to root out of an Englishman's mind
the notion that vice is delightful, and that abstention
from it is privation.
George Bernard Shaw

Vice is a creature of such hideous mind that the more
you see it the better you like it.
Finley Peter Dunne (1867-1936), American journalist and
humorist

How like herrings and onions our vices are in the
morning after we have committed them.
Samuel Taylor Coleridge (1772-1834)

What maintains one vice would bring up two children.
Benjamin Franklin

Society punishes not the vices of its members, but their
detection.
Countess of Blessington (1789-1849), novelist

The closer you get to vice, the less gilt and glamour you
find there is to it.
Sophie Tucker (1884-1966)

Permissiveness is simply removing the dust sheets from
our follies.
Edna O'Brien, Irish writer, Goodbye Baby and Amen

VIRGINITY

I thought of losing my virginity as a career move.
Madonna

All the evidence I've seen says that sex before marriage
isn't a good idea. Women are born virgins and sex is
something that is added to them. They are not
incomplete without it.
*Victoria Gillick, who campaigned unsuccessfully to prevent girls
under sixteen being prescribed the pill without their parents' consent*

I said it ten years ago that in ten years' time it would be
smart to be a virgin. Now everyone is back to virgins
again.
Barbara Cartland

What men desire is a virgin who is a whore.
Edward Dahlbert (1900-77)

Nature abhors a virgin – a frozen asset.
Clare Booth Luce

A simple maiden in her flower is worth a hundred
coats-of-arms.
Alfred, Lord Tennyson (1809-92), British poet, Lady Clara Vere
de Vere, *1833*

Although it is true that the hymen is often relaxed in
virgins, or broken and diminished by accidents
independent of all coition, such accidents are very rare,
and the absence of the hymen is assuredly a good
ground for strong suspicion.
T. Bell, British doctor, Kallogynomia, *1821*

Nothing is more horrible than the terror, the sufferings,
and the revulsion of a poor girl, ignorant of the facts of
life, who finds herself raped by a brute. As far as
possible we bring them up as saints, and then we hand
them over as if they were fillies.
George Sand (1804-76), French novelist, in a letter, 1843

The men you meet aren't naïve enough to expect virgins
but they certainly don't want to hear about the 'ghosts'
of your past life. Yet I can't imagine a man sticking
around much after two or three months if you hadn't
slept together.
Sacha Cowlam, Out of the Doll's House, *1988*

Sire, four virgins wait without. Without what? Without
food and clothing. Give them food and bring them in.
Anon, quoted in Only on Sundays, *Katherine Whithorn*

I hate a woman who seems to be hermetically sealed in
the lower regions.
Sydney Smith

It is one of the superstitions of the human mind to have
imagined that virginity could be a virtue.
Voltaire (1694-1778), French writer, Notebooks, *1778*

With regards to sexual relations, we should note that in
giving herself to sexual intercourse, the girl renounces
her honour. This is not, however, the case with men, for
they have yet another sphere for their ethical activity
beyond that of the family.
*Georg Hegel (1770-1831), German philosopher, referring to
unmarried girls,* The Philosophy of Right, *1821*

It will be quite sufficient for the memorial of my name
and for my glory if, when I die, an inscription be
engraved on a marble tomb, saying, 'Here lieth
Elizabeth, which reigned a virgin and died a virgin.'
*Queen Elizabeth I (1533-1603), in answer to a request by the
Speaker in the Lower House that she should marry*

Michael is not interested in girls and sex. He is
definitely still a virgin and doesn't believe he has missed
anything.
Chris Telvitt, tour manager for the singer Michael Jackson

V I R I L I T Y

There is no known way of increasing male sperm
production.
Dr Virginia E. Johnson

Virility is an illness which is best avoided.
Sir Nicholas Goodison, Chairman of the TSB Group plc

V I R T U E

Pleasure is something that you feel that you should
really enjoy, which is really virtuous, but you don't, and
sin is something that you're quite sure you shouldn't
enjoy but you do.
Ralph Wightman, speaking on Any Questions, *BBC Radio, 1961*

Virtue is its own revenge.
E. Y. Harburn (1898-1950)

Be virtuous and you will be eccentric.
Mark Twain

Most plain girls are virtuous because of the scarcity of opportunity to be otherwise.
Maya Angelou

What is virtue but the trade unionism of the married?
George Bernard Shaw, Don Juan, Man and Superman

There are few good women who do not tire of their role.
François, duc de La Rochefoucauld

I cannot love anyone if I hate myself. That is the reason why we feel so extremely uncomfortable in the presence of people who are noted for their special virtuousness, for they radiate an atmosphere of the torture they inflict on themselves. That is not a virtue but a vice.
Carl Jung (1875-1961), Swiss psychiatrist and writer

Assume a virtue, if you have it not.
William Shakespeare, Hamlet

Dost though think, because thou art virtuous, there shall be no more cake and ale?
William Shakespeare, Twelfth Night

Who can find a virtuous woman? For her price is far above rubies. The heart of her husband doth safely trust in her, so that he shall have no need of spoil. She will do him good and not evil all the days of her life.
Bible: *Proverbs 31: 10-12*

Most good women are hidden treasures who are only safe because nobody looks for them.
Dorothy Parker

Woman's virtue is a man's greatest invention.
Cornelia Otis Skinner (1901-89), stage actress

Virtue, like a dowerless beauty, has more admirers than followers.
Countess of Blessington

Virtue is not photogenic.
Kirk Douglas, American actor

Girls are sacrificed to family convenience, or else marry
to settle themselves in a superior rank . . . If some
widow did not now and then fall in love, love and
hymen would seldom meet, unless at a village church.
Mary Wollstonecraft *(1759-97), British writer,* Vindication of the
Rights of Women, *1792*

WEALTH

I think people still want to marry rich. Girls especially
. . . It's simple. Don't date poor boys. Go where the rich
are . . . You don't have to be rich to go where they go.
Sheilah Graham, *British-born American writer, the* Los Angeles
Times, *1974*

A gold rush is what happens when a line of chorus girls
spot a man with a bank roll.
From the film Klondike Annie, *1936*

WEATHER

I had a good eight inches last night.
Ulrika Johnsson, *TV weathergirl, talking about overnight
snowfalls*

I'm having problems with boyfriend withdrawal.
Ulrika Johnsson

Well, what happened last night, was it a storm?
Lisa Maxwell *to TV weathergirl Trish Williamson (the day after
the hurricane of 1987)*

Some people might wake up tomorrow and find they've
had an inch or two.
Michael Fish, *TV weatherman*

The strongest winds will be around the backside.
Bill Giles, *weatherman, discussing expected stormy weather in the
east of Britain*

Personally, I've got a very fine five-inch.
Patrick Moore, *astronomer*, Sky at night

WEDDINGS

Of all actions of a man's life his marriage does least concern other people; yet of all actions of our life it is more muddled with by other people.
John Sleden (1584-1654), English jurist and statesman

If it were not for the presents, an elopement would be preferable.
George Ade (1866-1944), American humorist and playwright

That is ever the way. 'Tis all jealousy to the bride and good wishes to the corpse.
J. M. Barrie (1860-1937), British playwright

The Wedding March always reminds me of the music played when soldiers go into battle.
Heinrich Heine (1797-1856), German poet and journalist

It has been said that a bride's attitude towards her betrothed can be summed up in three words: aisle, altar, hymn.
Frank Muir and Denis Norden, Oh, My Word

WIVES

You cannot pluck roses without fear of thorns, nor enjoy a fair wife without danger of horns.
Benjamin Franklin

I think of my wife and I think of Lot and I think of the lucky break he got.
William Cole, 'Marriage Couplet', from The Oxford Book of American Light Verse, 1979

The wife who submits to sexual intercourse against her wishes or desires, virtually commits suicide, while the husband who compels it, commits murder.
Victoria Claffin Woodhull (1838-1927), American feminist, political activist, writer and editor

She okays all my scripts. In my marital contract it's written that I can't do any sex scenes.
Dustin Hoffman on his wife

He who can't do any better goes to bed with his own wife.
Spanish proverb

Of course, I do have a slight advantage over the rest of
you. It helps in a pinch to be able to remind your bride
that you gave up a throne for her.
Duke of Windsor

Take my wife . . . please.
Henny Youngman

Many a man owes his success to his first wife and his
second wife to his success.
Jim Backus

Translations (like wives) are seldom faithful if they are
in the least attractive.
Roy Campbell (1901-57), South African poet, Poetry Review,
1949

The trouble with my wife is that she is a whore in the
kitchen and a cook in bed.
Geoffrey Gorer (1905-85), British writer and anthropologist,
Exploring the English Character, 1955

If a man stays away from his wife for seven years, the
law presumes the separation to have killed him; yet
according to our daily experience, it might well prolong
his life.
Lord Darling (1849-1936), British judge

The husband was a teetotaller, there was no other
woman, and the conduct complained of was that he
had drifted into the habit of winding up every meal by
taking out his false teeth and hurling them at his wife.
Arthur Conan Doyle (1856-1930), British writer, A Case of
Identity, 1892

Wives are young men's mistresses, companions for
middle age, and old men's nurses.
Francis Bacon

I chose my wife, as she did her wedding-gown, not for a
fine glossy surface, but such qualities as would wear
well.
Oliver Goldsmith

He will hold thee, when his passion shall have spent its
novel force, something better than his dog, a little
dearer than his horse.
Alfred, Lord Tennyson

One can always recognise women who trust their husbands; they look so thoroughly unhappy.
Oscar Wilde

The woman who cannot evolve a good lie in defence of the man she loves is unworthy the name of wife.
Elbert Hubbard

Good wives and private soldiers should be ignorant.
William Wycherley (1640-1716), English dramatist

If a woman has her Ph.D. in physics, has mastered in Quantum theory, plays flawless Chopin, was once a cheerleader, and is now married to a man who plays baseball, she will forever be 'Former Cheerleader married to Star Athlete'.
Maryanne Ellson Simmons, wife of Milwaukee Brewers catcher Ted Simmons

Many men owe their success to their wives. I owe my wife to my success.
Anonymous millionaire

Reading someone else's newspaper is like sleeping with someone else's wife. Nothing seems to be precisely in the right place, and when you find what you are looking for, it is not clear then how to respond to one.
Malcolm Bradbury, Stepping Westward, 1965

Never feel remorse for what you have thought about your wife; she has thought much worse things about you.
Jean Rostand (1894-1977), French biologist and writer, Le Mariage, 1927

When a man opens a car door for his wife, it's either a new car or a new wife.
Prince Philip, the consort of Queen Elizabeth II, 1988

If the husband is the criminal, he escapes with little or no injury either fame or fortune. If the wife be the criminal, the perceptions of the world and her incapacity to make honourable provision for herself, compel her to join the ranks of prostitutes.
T. Bell, British doctor, Kalogynomia, 1821

Your wives are your field: go in, therefore, to your field as you will.
Koran, seventh century

WOMANHOOD

You sometimes have to answer a woman according to her womanishness, just as you have to answer a fool according to his folly.
George Bernard Shaw

Women in drudgery knew they must be one of four: whores, artists, saints and wives.
Murial Rukeyser (1913-80), American poet, 'Beast in View', Wreath of Women, *1944*

I get the impression that she loves life, and people too . . . she doesn't write like a man but like a 100 per cent woman, a female, sometimes, a 'bitch'. In many ways she is more forthright, more honest, more daring than most male authors.
Henry Miller, the New York Times, *on* Fear of Flying *by Erica Jong, 1974*

Probably the most successful mode of rearing girls, so as to bring them to the full perfection of womanhood, is to retard the period of puberty as much as possible . . . It is the duty therefore, of the mother to enjoin on her daughter the frequent use of cold baths, free exercise in the open air, or in cool, well-ventilated rooms, to provide plain and digestible diet for her, and to insist on abstinence from hot tea and coffee.
E. H. Ruddock, The Common Diseases of Women, *1888*

You may marry or you may not. In today's world that is no longer the big question for women. Those who grab on to men so that they can collapse with relief, spend the rest of their days shining up their status symbol and figure they never have to reach, stretch, learn, grow, face dragons or make a living again, are the ones to be pitied. They, in my opinion, are the unfulfilled ones.
Helen Gurley Brown, American writer, Sex and the Single Girl, *1963*

The nicest women in our 'society' are raving sex maniacs. But being just awfully nice they don't, of course, descend to fucking – that's uncouth – rather they make love, commune by means of their bodies and establish sensual rapport.
Valerie Solanas, American writer, Born Female, *1968*

She takes just like a woman, yes, she does
she makes love just like a woman, yes, she does
and she aches just like a woman
but she breaks just like a little girl.
Bob Dylan, *American singer and songwriter*, Just Like a Woman,
1966

To be a liberated woman is to renounce the desire of
being a sex object or a baby girl. It is to acknowledge
that the Cinderella-Prince Charming story is a child's
fairy tale.
Clare Boothe Luce *(1903-87), American politician, journalist and
playwright, 1974*

WOMEN

Women are like banks, boy. Breaking and entering is a
serious business.
Joe Orton *(1933-67), Entertaining Mr Sloane, 1964*

Aren't women prudes if they don't and prostitutes if
they do?
Kate Millett, *American writer, lecturer and sculptor*

With women, I've got a long bamboo pole with a
leather loop on the end of it. I slip the loop around their
necks so they can't get away or come too close. Like
catching snakes.
Marlon Brando, *American actor*

What do you think: women – a mistake? Or did He do
it to us on purpose?
Jack Nicholson *in the film* The Witches of Eastwick *(screenplay by
Michael Cristofer, from the novel by John Updike)*

A beautiful woman who gives pleasure to men serves
only to frighten the fish when she jumps in the water.
Kwang Tse

God did it on purpose so that we may love you men
instead of laughing at you.
Mrs Patrick *Campbell (1865-1940), British actress, in reply to a
male acquaintance who asked why women seem to have no sense of
humour*

You don't know a woman until you have had a letter
from her.
Ada Leverson *(1862-1933), English writer*

Women are like dogs really. They love like dogs, a little insistently. And they like to fetch and carry and come back wistfully after hard words, and learn rather easily to carry a basket.
Mary Roberts Rinehart

Being a woman is of special interest only to aspiring male transsexuals. To actual women, it is simply a good excuse not to play football.
Fran Lebowitz, American journalist

I should like to know what is the proper function of women, if it is not to make reasons for husbands to stay at home, and still stronger reasons for bachelors to go out.
George Eliot (Mary Ann Evans, 1819-80), English novelist

There are two kinds of women: those who want power in the world, and those who want power in bed.
Jacqueline Kennedy Onassis

Behind almost every woman you have ever heard of stands a man who has let her down.
Naomi Bliven, American writer

A woman can look both moral and exciting . . . if she also looks as if it was quite a struggle.
Edna Ferber (1887-1968), American writer

A liberated woman is one who has sex before marriage and a job after.
Gloria Steinem

Nine times out of ten a woman had better show more affection than she feels.
Jane Austen

We have drugs to make women speak, but none to keep them silent.
Anatole France

There are three intolerable things in life – cold coffee, lukewarm champagne, and overexcited women.
Orson Wells

Both women and melons are best when fairly ripe.
Spanish proverb

All women are trollops.
French proverb

Watch out for women's tricks!
Libretto of The Magic Flute, *opera by* W.A. Mozart

Woman is the wrath of Zeus.
Greek proverb

The costliest women are the ones who cost nothing.
Alfred de Musset (1810-57), French poet and playwright

A woman uses her intelligence to find reasons to
support her intuition.
G. K. Chesterton

Women are one of the Almighty's enigmas to prove to
men that He knows more than they do.
Ellen Glasgow (1873-1945), American novelist

Women are most fascinating between the ages of thirty-
five and forty after they have won a few races and
know how to pace themselves. Since few ever pass
forty, maximum fascination can continue indefinitely.
Christian Dior (1905-57), French couturier

There's nothing so similar to one poodle dog as another
poodle dog, and that goes for women too.
Pablo Picasso

A lady is known by the product she endorses.
Ogden Nash, American poet, First Families Move Over

Women should be obscene and not heard.
John Lennon

Women never know when the curtain has fallen. They
always want a sixth act, and as soon as the interest of
the play is entirely over, they propose to continue it.
Oscar Wilde, The Picture of Dorian Gray

It was a woman who drove me to drink, and I never
had the courtesy to thank her for it.
W. C. Fields (1879-1946), American actor and screenwriter

A woman is but an animal, and an animal not of the
highest order.
Edmund Burke (1729-97), British politician and writer

A pessimist is a man who thinks all women are bad. An
optimist is one who hopes they are.
Chauncey Depew

There are lots of good women who, when they get to heaven, will watch to see if the Lord goes out nights.
Ed Howe

I'm just a person trapped inside a woman's body.
Elaine Boosler

A woman, especially if she has the misfortune of knowing anything, should conceal it as well as she can.
Jane Austen (1775-1817), Northanger Abbey

You know women as well as I do. They are only willing when you compel them, but after that they're as enthusiastic as you are.
Jean Giraudoux (1882-1944), French dramatist, Tiger at the Gates, *1935*

Girls are taught from childhood that any exhibition of sexual feeling is unwomanly and intolerable; they also learn from an early age that if a woman makes a mistake it is upon her and upon her alone that social punishment will descend.
Mary Scharlieb (1845-1930), British gynaecological surgeon and writer, The Seven Ages of Women

Solitary women exhibit pseudo-masculine efficiency, a determined practical competence which they might expect or demand from a husband if only they had one.
Anthony Storr, British psychiatrist, Human Aggression, *1968*

She is Venus when she smiles; but she's Juno when she walks, and Minerva when she talks.
Ben Jonson (1573-1637), English dramatist

I am a source of satisfaction to him, a nurse, a piece of furniture, a woman – nothing more.
Sophie Tolstoy (1844-1919), Russian writer, A Diary of Tolstoy's Wife, 1860-91, *1863*

And a woman is only a woman, but a good cigar is a smoke.
Rudyard Kipling (1865-1936), Indian-born British writer, The Betrothed

The ten properties of a woman:
YE. I. Is to be a merry chere
YE. II. To be well placed
YE. III. To have a broad forhead
YE. IIII. To have broad buttocks
YE. V. To be hard of ward
YE. VI To be easy to leap upon
YE. VII. To be good at long journey
YE. VIII. To be well sturring under a man
YE. VIIII. To be always busy wt ye mouth
YE. X. Ever to be chewing on ye bridle.
Fitzherbert's Boke of Husbandry, 1568

Nature placed the female testicles internally . . . woman
is a most arrogant and extremely intractable animal;
and she would be worse if she came to realise that she is
no less perfect and no less fit to wear breeches than man
. . . I believe that is why nature, while endowing her
with what is necessary for procreation, did so in such a
way as to keep her from perceiving and ascertaining her
sufficient perfection.
P. Borgarucci, *Italian anatomist*

God created woman. And boredom did indeed cease
from that moment – but many other things ceased as
well! Woman was God's second mistake.
Friedrich Nietzsche *(1844-1900)*

Menstruating women carry with them a poison that
could kill an infant in its cradle.
St Albert The Great *(c.1206-80), German Dominican bishop and
philosopher*

It is an undoubted fact that meat spoils when touched
by menstruating women.
Quoted in the British Medical Journal, *1878*

The judgment of God upon your sex endures even
today; and with it inevitably endures your position of
criminal at the bar of justice. You are the gateway to
the devil.
Tertullian, *Roman theologian*

A woman's place is in the wrong.
James Thurber *(1894-1961), American humorist and illustrator*

Woman are not much but they are the best other sex we have. When children cease to be altogether desirable women cease to be altogether necessary.
John Langdon-Davies (1897-1971), British author

There is only one real tragedy in a woman's life: the fact that her past is always her lover, and her future invariably her husband.
Oscar Wilde

A woman's whole life is a history of the affections.
Washington Irving (1783-1859), American author

It is assumed that a woman must wait motionless, until she is wooed. That is how the spider waits for the fly.
George Bernard Shaw

Woman reduces us all to a common denominator.
George Bernard Shaw

The fickleness of the women whom I love is only equalled by the infernal constancy of the women who love me.
George Bernard Shaw

Many women still feel it's not their right to look at erotic photos of men. They also have trouble finding the words to express their sexuality. We're going to have to create a new language.
Pauline Brown, editor of For Women *magazine*

Once a woman has given her heart you can never get rid of the rest of her body.
Sir John Vanbrugh (1664-1726), The Relapse, *1697*

If you really worship women they'll forgive you everything, even if your balls are dropping off.
Lawrence Durrell, British writer

Anyone who says he can see through women is missing a lot.
Groucho Marx, Quote and Unquote

A womane is a worthy wyght
she serveth a man both daye and nyght,
therto she puttyth alle her myght,
and yet she hathe but care and woo.
Anon, Medieval English Lyrics *(ed. R. T. Davies), fifteenth century*

There are two kinds of women – goddesses and doormats.
Pablo Picasso

W H A T   D O   W O M E N
W A N T ?

Despite my thirty years of research into the feminine soul, I have not yet been able to answer ... the great question that has never been answered: what does a woman want?
Sigmund Freud

Any idiot would know women's needs are simple. All we want is your basic millionaire/brain surgeon/ criminal lawyer/great dancer who pilots his own Lear Jet and owns oceanfront property. On the other hand, things being what they are today, most of us will settle for a guy who holds down a steady job and isn't carrying an infectious disease.
Linda Sunshine

Women want men, careers, money, children, friends, luxury, comfort, independence, freedom, respect, love and a three-dollar pantyhose that won't run.
Phyllis Diller

What this woman wants, with all due respect to Sigmund Freud, is for men to stop asking that question and to realise that women are human beings, not some alien species. They want the same things men want.
Diane White

Women want family life that glitters and is stable. They don't want some lump spouse watching ice hockey in the late hours of his eighteenth beer. They want a family that is so much fun and is so smart that they look forward to Thanksgiving rather than regarding it with a shudder. That's the glitter part. The stable part is, obviously, they don't want to be one bead on a long necklace of wives. They want, just like men, fun, love, fame, money and power, and equal pay for equal work.
Carolyn See

Exactly what men want: love, money, excitement, pleasure, happiness, fulfilling work – and sometimes a child who will say 'I love you'.
Joyce Brothers

I'd like to own Texas and lease Colorado.
Rita Mae Brown

Freedom from pain, security, creature comforts, and an end to loneliness. When you get down to the basics, it's still the same old story, a fight for love and glory.
Alice Kahn

Vain man is apt to think we were merely intended for the world's propagation and to keep its human inhabitants sweet and clean; but, by their leaves, had we the same literature he would find our brains as fruitful as our bodies.
Hannah Woolley, Gentlewoman's Companion, *1675*

That's a dumb question: only a fraud like Freud could make a problem out of an opportunity.
Edward Abbey, American author, on being asked what women want

Implicit obedience.
Horace Rumpole, from Rumpole of the Bailey *by John Mortimer*

Men.
Malcolm Forbes

Money, power, love, sex (until they get married), adulation, children and control. Of these, children cause the most trouble. Women also want equal rights and equal pay for equal work, and I agree with them 100 per cent, though on some days it is hard to figure out how a species that controls 97 per cent of the money and all the pussy can be downtrodden.
Larry L. King

Do you know what the women in this town are really after? They want jewels in their bank vaults, Chanel clothes in their wardrobe, a Porsche in their garage, a tiger in their bed – and an ass of a husband who pays for it all.
Shobha De, Indian novelist

Oh Charles – a woman needs certain things. She needs
to be loved, wanted, cherished, sought after, wooed,
flattered, cossetted, pampered. She needs sympathy,
affection, devotion, understanding, tenderness,
infatuation, adulation, idolatry – that isn't much to ask,
Charles.
Round the Horne, *by Barry Took and Marty Feldman, BBC Radio,*
1966

What else do they want in life but to be as attractive as
possible to men? Do not all their trimmings and
cosmetics have this end in view, and all their baths,
fittings, creams, scents as well – and all those arts of
making up, painting, and fashioning the face, eyes and
skin? Just so. And by what other sponsor are they better
recommended to men than by folly?
Erasmus *(1467-1535), Dutch humanist, scholar and writer,* In
Praise of Folly, *1509*

I like them on their knees, in the kitchen, doing the
dusting. In return, I feed them, wine them, make them
laugh, occasionally – and give them a punch on the nose
and a good kicking when they need it. They're happier
that way. They feel secure.
Oliver Reed, *actor*

WOMAN'S ROLE

It is a man's place to rule, and a woman's to yield. He
must be held up as the head of the house, and it is her
duty to bend so unmurmuringly to his wishes, that the
rest of the household will follow her example, and treat
him with the due respect his sex demands.
Sarah Ann Sewell, *British writer and social critic,* Woman and the
Times We Live In, *1869*

As a general rule, a modest woman seldom desires any
sexual gratification for herself. She submits to her
husband, but only to please him; and, but for the desire
of maternity, would rather be relieved from his
attentions.
W. Acton, The Functions and Disorders of the Reproductive
Organs, *1865*

Maids must be wives and mothers, to fulfil the entire
and holiest end of woman's being.
Fanny Kemble (1809-93), British actress, writer and poet,
Woman's Heart

X - R A T E D

All women think they're ugly, even pretty women. A
man who understood this could fuck more women than
Don Giovanni. They all think their cunts are ugly . . .
they all find fault with their figures . . . even models
and actresses, even the women you think are so
beautiful that they have nothing to worry about, do
worry all the time.
Erica Jong

Nobody, including the Supreme Court, knows what
obscenity is.
Norman Dorsen

I never trust a man unless I've got his pecker in my
pocket.
Lyndon B. Johnson (1908-73), former American president

Yes, I went to see one the other night called *Jilly* [about
a girl who] goes to the dentist for a fillin' and a drillin',
and frankly I enjoyed it a lot more than I did *Heartburn*
with Jack Nicholson and Meryl Streep, for a couple of
reasons. One, Meryl Streep is a dog. She's a good
actress, but the girl is a dog. She reminds me a lot of
Cordie Mae Poovey, a girl I went to high school with.
She played a great trumpet, but goddamn she was ugly.
Lewis Grizzard, on being asked if he watched X-rated movies

I always wanted to be an animated character. And
basically that's what I do now. I'm kind of an X-rated
Cinderella.
Cher

A question asked in a Surrey school exam went: 'Why
do cocks crow early every morning?'
A twelve-year-old replied: 'My dad says they have to
make the most of it while the hens are asleep.'
Anon, quoted in the Peterborough Daily Telegraph, *1983*

After four martinis, my husband turns into a disgusting
beast. And after the fifth, I pass out altogether.
Anon

An adult western is where the hero still kisses his horse
at the end only now he worries about it.
Milton Berle, Variety *magazine, 1978*

The word 'fuck' appears thirty times, the word 'cunt'
fourteen times, the word 'balls' thirteen times, 'shit' six
times, 'arse' and 'piss' three times apiece.
Mervyn Griffiths-Jones, *British prosecuting counsel, at the trial
for obscenity of D. H. Lawrence's novel,* Lady Chatterley's Lover,
1960

I doubt if there are any rational people to whom the
word 'fuck' would be particularly diabolical, or totally
forbidden.
Kenneth Tynan, *British critic speaking on BBC TV, 1965*

To be human is to be fucked. To know that you're
fucked right off the bat.
Murray Schisgal, *American writer,* Playboy *magazine, 1975*

There are times when I like sex and times when I don't.
When I'm in the mood for it, I like nothing better. But I
don't enjoy cruelty. I hate it when somebody I don't
know comes out wearing a rubber diving suit with a
battleship in one hand and a jar of vaseline in the other.
Barbara Hutton, *actress*

YOUTH

They think youth has got him where he is, beside me.
This isn't so. I think it was his fart that fascinated me
first, and the way he commented on it. No one that I
was involved with at the time ever acknowledged their
farts. 'Smell this,' he said, and gave me a bisto sniff. 'I
always think the best have something of mushroom on
toast about them – don't you?' And we hadn't even
been to bed – it was while we were both undressing.
Molly Parkin *on her younger husband*

How absurd and delicious it is to be in love with
someone younger than yourself. Everyone should try it.
Barbara Pym

My girlfriend has married an old man;
I have married a younger.
Her old man is witty, sexy and strong;
mine's the same. But mine will last longer.
Molly Parkin

Perhaps at fourteen every boy should be in love with
some ideal women to put on a pedestal and worship. As
he grows up, of course, he will put her on a pedestal the
better to view her legs.
Barry Norman, British cinema critic and broadcaster, The Listener
magazine, 1978

Index